Radical Church

A Call to Rediscover the Radical Roots of the Christian Faith

John Caldwell

EP BOOKS
1st Floor Venture House, 6 Silver Court, Watchmead,
Welwyn Garden City, UK, AL7 1TS

web: http://www.epbooks.org

e-mail: sales@epbooks.org

EP Books are distributed in the USA by:
JPL Distribution
3741 Linden Avenue Southeast
Grand Rapids, MI 49548
E-mail: orders@jpldistribution.com
Tel: 877.683.6935

British Library Cataloguing in Publication Data available

ISBN 978-1-78397-182-4

Each generation requires a fresh evaluation and application of the foundational principles of the gospel. That is what John Caldwell has provided in this book: a recovery of the roots of our Christian faith in God and his Word. Written from the perspective of someone who was radically transformed by grace, John wants us to confront the prevailing culture of our day with nothing less than the gospel of Jesus Christ. It is a message we need to hear.

Rev Dr Iain D. Campbell Minister, Point Free Church, Isle of Lewis; author, and editor of *The Monthly Record*.

'Instead of calling people from darkness to light, we are inviting people to come and sit in the dark,' summarizes well the concern of this excellent book. The church today is trying to reach the culture by increasingly becoming like the culture rather than pointing people to the Way, the Truth and the Life. *Radical Church* is a clear call to God's people to return to the Scriptures for God's paradigm for our lives and churches.

Dr. Gary Gilley, Pastor of Southern View Chapel, and author of a number of books, including '*This Little Church Went to Market*'.

Radical Church issues an uncompromising challenge to the church 'to function as a lighthouse not a dimmer switch' by engaging in what the author rightly describes as the 'tremendously difficult and dangerous call to be both faithful to the truth and to engage the world'.

Peter J. Grainger, Director of '2 Timothy 4' and former pastor of Charlotte Chapel, Edinburgh.

In this fresh, fast-flowing and very readable narrative, the author reveals how the Western Church has to a considerable degree lost both its relevance and vitality in an increasingly anti-Christian culture. The answer, he passionately believes, is not compromising to culture, but faithfulness to Christ, and he calls the Church back to its biblical roots, with its emphasis on the Cross. A pertinent call to radical, Christ-centred living.

Tom Lennie, revival historian, author of '*Glory in the Glen*' and '*Land of Many Revivals*'.

In *Radical Church*, John Caldwell enters the room, names and shames a whole herd of elephants and offers robust solutions for the current crisis facing the broad evangelical movement. He unpacks the concept of radicalism and comes to the conclusion that the agents of change are not to be found in either the effete banalities of post-evangelicalism or the cringe-worthy offerings of the best-selling celebrity evangelicals but in an older, deeper, truly radical philosophy emerging from the teaching of that quintessential radical: Jesus of Nazareth.

This is truly a 95 Theses for contemporary evangelicalism.

Rev David Meredith, Mission Director, Free Church of Scotland

The Church in Scotland (and in the West) is in danger of sleepwalking into disaster. John Caldwell issues a clarion call for us to wake up and smell the coffee. Whether you stand in a pulpit or sit in a pew, John wants you to be clear on the fundamentals of the faith, the biblical, historic gospel of Jesus Christ. Each 'Radical' chapter takes the reader back to the foundations. Labels without meaning are inadequate and frankly dishonest. Much that purports to be 'Christian' or 'Evangelical' is built not on a sound biblical foundation but some concession with reason or whatever cultural phenomenon is currently in vogue. Wake up Christians because while you slumber your enemies are wide awake and active. It is a pleasure to have John sitting in front of me as a student of theology, it is more gratifying still to know that he is practising and preaching that of which he writes.

Bob Akroyd, Professor of Systematic Theology, Edinburgh Theological Seminary

Dedication

To Martin—for taking the time to disciple a new Christian, and teaching, not only the importance of the gospel and the scriptures, but also the church—'which is the pillar and foundation of the truth.' (1 Timothy 3:15)

Acknowledgements

I need to thank several people for their input and support of this book. Thanks, must first of all be expressed to my wife Laura, who supported the writing of this manuscript in the midst of a major relocation—timing is everything! Thanks to David Robertson for writing the foreword— David's apologetic evangelism is an inspiration, to have him write the foreword is a great honour. Thanks also to Tom Lennie and Iain D. Campbell, not only for their endorsement, but also for their constructive feedback on the content—I hope the finished product reflects their wise input. Thanks, is also due to Gary Gilley—whose own writings on the church have impacted me deeply, were it not for his writing, this book would never have been written. Further thanks to Peter Grainger, David Meredith and Bob Akroyd for their kind endorsements. My only regret about this book is that I hadn't sat in Bob's Systematic Theology classes prior to writing this book— had I done so, this book would be a lot better than it is—and a lot longer! I also want to thank Graham at

Evangelical Press for his support, right from the start, when this book was all but a proposal, he caught the vision for it. Thanks are due to EP's editor, Trudy Kinloch who has whipped a rough draft into great shape—not to mention bearing patiently with several late changes—thanks again Trudy! Thanks are also due to several people that I haven't named, who read the early drafts, offered encouragement and highlighted typos—all of you have contributed to this work in your own way—your help was a great support. Finally, and most importantly, I want to thank the God and Father of my Lord Jesus Christ who took me out of the pit, set my feet on a rock and put a new song in my mouth. I never cease to be amazed at how he has worked in my life—I pray this book is used to bring him glory, strengthen his church, and reach the lost.

Contents

Foreword

'For too long the western church has occupied a throne and has abandoned the cross. The church has reigned as king instead of bowing as a servant.'

John Caldwell's statement is not new. In fact there is very little in this wee book that is new. You can find more detailed analysis of current cultural trends, contemporary church issues, historical developments and in-depth theology elsewhere. What you will not find, and what *is* new, is that all these things are brought together in this one book in a manner which addresses the needs of the churches today and which is accessible to the vast majority of people.

John's basic thesis is one that I would totally agree with. One of the reasons that we set up *Solas Centre for Public Christianity* was precisely because we identified the same trends that John notices. With his social and varied ecclesiastical background he is well able to comment from both an insider's and outsider's perspective, on the confused state of the Church of Jesus Christ in the United Kingdom today.

Confused is perhaps the best word to describe what is going on. There is a great deal of confusion in the general society about God, the Bible, humanity, morality and ethics. It seems as though the foundations have been destroyed and people wonder what can they do? What is even more disturbing is that the church seems to reflect the trends within the culture and therefore ends up being even more confused. Perhaps we really are at a stage where God is judging the nation and letting us go our own way? We have become the blind leading the blind.

None of this is new. God's church has often existed within confused and apparently declining situations. But God in his mercy does not leave us alone, which would indeed be the ultimate judgement. He sends his word, and he sends those who proclaim his word. John Caldwell is such a person. His analysis in this book of the contemporary church scene in the United Kingdom (and therefore applicable in the wider Western world) is insightful, depressing, and yet somehow stimulating and encouraging. This is not an academic thesis looking at the sociological aspects of religion from the safe vantage point of an armchair in an ivory tower. Nor is it the story of one particular work of God in a particular location at a particular time. This is a view from the battlefield, which takes a broad sweep over the whole contemporary situation.

What is especially helpful about this small book is that it takes a number of disciplines and applies them in a practical way to the current church situation. John notes that in reaction to a sinful, competitive denominationalism, evangelical Christians seem to have thrown out the baby with the bathwater. We have exchanged one mess for another. Reflecting the culture more than Scriptures, we have ended up with a sinful competitive networking based on dominant personalities and advertising branding. The branding of the church is neither radical nor biblical.

Of course there are those of us who are long enough in the tooth to find ourselves cringing whenever we hear the word radical. Every new program, every new work of God is deemed to be 'radical'. I find myself yawning and switching off when I am told to read, watch or support the latest radical initiative from the latest in-vogue Christian organization. If you have to say you are 'edgy' you are not! What I love about John's book is that it is radical, precisely because it does not seek to provide us with something new. It points us instead to Scripture, the basics of the Christian faith and the lessons we can learn from our own history.

What is more radical than the cross? And yet how many contemporary evangelicals either do not understand or water down or even deny the atonement? And it's not just the foundational issues of the cross, the person and work of Christ, or the inspiration and sufficiency of the Scriptures, which are under attack. It is also how we apply them, and how the church lives out the doctrines of the Scriptures in the contemporary world whose world view is so antithetical to them.

Whilst there are Christians who will argue that what

we need to focus on is evangelism, others who argue that mercy ministry is the way ahead, and still others who want to emphasize prayer, Bible teaching and personal devotion; far too often the church in its various manifestations is either forgotten, sidelined or dismissed. John's 'radical' notion is that all of these things matter and that all of them come together in the church. In order to communicate the gospel we need therefore to work out, not only what the gospel is, but also how we live it out in the community of the church.

As you read this book there are things that you will say Amen to! There are other things that you will question or disagree with, and gaps that you will want to fill in. But one thing is absolutely sure—every single chapter of this book deals with issues which are vital to the well-being and health of the whole church in today's society. It will benefit you enormously to prayerfully read through and think about these issues.

Just as 'radical' is an overused and often cringeworthy word, so 'conversation' often shares the same fate. But in this instance the word conversation is very appropriate. My hope and prayer is that this book will stimulate many conversations which cause us to turn to the Lord, the head of the church, and ask him what he wants. May it be that we will be encouraged to be faithful to his Word, to be salt and light in a society which rejects that word, and to once again see the renewal, revival and re-formation of the church in our societies.

Christ is on the throne. We are not. We do not tell him what he should be doing with his church. We just simply say 'speak Lord for your servants are listening'. And then pray that he would give us strength and grace to be doers as well as hearers of the word.

The words of the Psalmist should be the prayer all who read and understand this book:

Psalm 80

> 14 Return to us, God Almighty!
>   Look down from heaven and see!
>   Watch over this vine,
> 15   the root your right hand has planted,
>   the son you have raised up for yourself.
> 16 Your vine is cut down, it is burned with fire;
>   at your rebuke your people perish.
> 17 Let your hand rest on the man at your right hand,
>   the son of man you have raised up for yourself.
> 18 Then we will not turn away from you;
>   revive us, and we will call on your name.
> 19 Restore us, Lord God Almighty;
>   make your face shine on us,
>   that we may be saved.

David Robertson
St Peter's Free Church
Solas Centre for Public Christianity
August 2016

Introduction

In Scotland, 18 years ago, I was living a life which was at odds with mainstream society and the law. A constant cocktail of narcotics and alcohol had rendered me unfit for work. I lived in a constant drunken state. Most nights on the drink led to either a pub fight or a street fight. I landed in a jail cell twice for a combination of breaching the peace, assault and vandalism. As I've recounted in my first book, *Christ, the Cross and the Concrete Jungle*—my life was completely turned around by the gospel of Jesus Christ. Scotland has often been referred to as 'The Land of the Book'—a reference to the rich Christian heritage. As I turned to the Book, the Book worked its magic. Instead of living on benefits, and abusing the system; I work full time and pay my taxes. Instead of living life drunk, I live life sober. Instead of drifting from one sexual encounter to another, I'm happily married and the father of two amazing sons. Instead of cursing Christianity, I now preach and teach Christianity. My children, instead of growing up in a godless environment, are growing up learning the ways of

God. Yet here's the irony—in turning back to the Book that once underpinned the social fabric of the land, I once again find myself living a life which is becoming increasingly at odds with mainstream society and the law. It is not outside the realms of possibility that I could, in the future, find myself in jail, for living my life according to the Book, and teaching my children to live according to the Book, and calling society to turn to the Book.

What's happened? Whilst Jesus has been saving sinners, like me, to himself, society has been transitioning away from the faith that once defined our culture. Almost overnight we have seen a dramatic shift in our culture. The dramatic shift is this: to live and speak according to the values and customs, that were once taken for granted, is to live and speak as a radical extremist. What was a cultural norm yesterday, is a cultural taboo today.

I grew up in the central-belt in Scotland between the 80s and 90s. We were a Roman Catholic family, we attended a Roman Catholic School, and we lived in a 'diverse' community—a community divided between Catholics and Protestants. Despite the sectarian divide, the reality is, most of us had more in common, than we had differences. Both sides grew up with a church connection, most of us were baptized as infants, most of us had a shared sense of right and wrong (even when we didn't comply with it!). In my early primary school years, there was a religious and moral coherence woven through life. Church, school, and home life shared the same moral and religious framework.

Today things are very different. Just a few weeks ago I had my two sons (who were 6 and 7) baptized in our local

Presbyterian church. (It wasn't a believer's baptism). I shared the pictures on social media for friends and family to see. Somehow the picture ended up on a Secular Society discussion forum, accompanying an angry thread, full of outraged atheists expressing their disgust at my children being baptized because it was a breach of their individual human rights to have such a ceremony inflicted upon them. It suddenly struck me, something once considered a cultural norm (the baptism of a child) is now something very radical. It's a statement of rebellion to the secularism that wants to dominate every sphere of life—from the market place to the home. Baptism is an act of defiance that says to the secularist worldview—*You don't reign here, Jesus does.*

What we are seeing in the west, is a shift of worldviews. We need to understand though that the new secular humanism which has replaced the Judeo-Christian worldview, is not neutral territory. Despite its foundational dogmas such as freedom, equality, tolerance and respect, the reality is that the new secularism is a dictatorial philosophy that leaves no room for non-conformity. This god of equality will not share its throne with diversity—all must comply, all must conform.

Two recent examples demonstrate this. In one case, a UK judge was sacked because he believed that it was more beneficial for adopted children to be placed 'with a mother and father'. The judge argued, 'As a magistrate, I have to act on the evidence before me and quite simply, I believe that there is not sufficient evidence to convince me that placing a child in the care of a same-sex couple can be as holistically beneficial to a child as placing them with a mum and dad as God and nature intended.'[1] The magistrate was sacked on the basis that his views were considered to be evidence that he was biased and prejudiced against same-sex couples who wish to adopt.

This kind of situation is being replicated all over the western world. The reality is, the push for 'equal marriage', and the change in law to redefine marriage, has ultimately led to a censoring of the traditional view of marriage. It's clear that the two views cannot exist freely. When governments decide to allow same-sex partners to 'marry', the consequence is that they create problems for those who still view marriage in historic, natural, and biblical terms. The new equality dogma may not condemn people for *thinking* what they want about marriage, but if these same people try to live or speak about it—there are social, political and legal consequences. This basically means that faith is being forced into the private corners of our lives. It's the great reversal. Sex and sexuality, once a private thing, are now public matters, and faith and ethics are now being forced into the privacy of our thought-life. Secularism silences conscience.

The second example is the backlash that an Equality Minister received when it came to light that she had voted against gay marriage. No sooner had she been appointed the role of Equality Minister than the critics began their social media attack, 'how can you get a job on equality when you're against same-sex marriages?'[2] asked one online critic. Of course, the question is rhetorical. It's not a question, it's a statement. If it were a question, it could open up an important discussion, but the new secularists don't want debate, they want dogma. They don't want dissent, they want conformity. The message seems clear—if you want a seat at the table in society, you need to conform to the new orthodoxy. You need to accept the new dogma. How far this will actually go is yet to be seen. But the way it is looking at the moment, Christians will either have to accept silence or seclusion. Any Christian who hopes to stand by their convictions, and customs that were up until recently considered to be social norms, risks being censored, sacked or sued.

The battleground is not just in the area of sexual ethics, and the warzone is not restricted to the market place; the fight is for the foundations of the Christian faith, and the conflict extends to the church. The church is not just engaged in battle with the enemy without; the church is also at war with the enemy within.

The rise of aggressive atheism ('there's no God and I hate him'); moral relativism (there is no absolute truth, except the absolute truth that there is no absolute truth); Inclusive Fundamentalism (everyone is welcome, except those who disagree with us) and Judgemental-Non-Judgementalism (how dare you judge our judgements!) have all made a dent, not only on the psyche of society, but also the life of the church. As anti-biblical worldviews have grown stronger, the church has grown weaker.

Consequently, much of the Christian church is an embarrassment. Denominational leaders and Christian pastors, desperate for a seat at the table, are pathetically trying to straddle two worlds. The most glaring and obvious example of this is the recent debacle within the Church of Scotland, who, in their 2015 General Assembly, 'adopted a position which maintains a traditional view of marriage between a man and woman, but allows individual congregations to "opt out" if they wish to appoint a minister or a deacon in a same-sex civil partnership.'[3]

Such contradictory and capitulating cowardice is simply one symptom of the times. But it's not only the national church. We see similar political manoeuvring within evangelicalism too. Pastors, afraid to lose their 'influence' duck and dive questions from the media with political expertise. Given an opportunity to speak to parliament, many evangelical leaders stand up and spout words about 'human compassion', 'God's love', and the 'inclusive and diverse nature of the church'. What do they mean? Who knows. But this much is clear, many leaders are choosing the path of ambiguity, rather than sounding out a clear, convicting message. Consequently, the church is losing its voice because the church has lost its spine.

It seems to me, there are three options available to the church today: compromise and die; hide in the trenches and die a little more slowly; or hold fast to truth, engage the world and see what God does. Granted, the last option is the most difficult. It's far easier to play the 'relevant' card and redefine our faith in a way that fits with the secularist culture—all the while preaching bland, powerless platitudes about God's love for everyone as the basis for hope. Anyone can do that. Try to please everyone but God and receive a pat on the back from the world whilst doing it. But beware, for those who take this path have already had their reward: 'Woe to you, when all people speak well of you, for so their fathers did to the false prophets.' (Luke 6:26)

Or we can batten down the hatches, 'hold the fort' until he comes, desperately try to hold on to the few church members we have, and let the world go to hell. Okay, we might shout over our walls with loud tannoys, and pat ourselves on the back for being a faithful evangelist— but that's not exactly the incarnational model we see demonstrated in the life of Jesus Christ. Jesus has not called us to hide in a holy huddle, he has called us to leave the comfort zone: 'Behold, I am sending you out as sheep in the midst of wolves, so be wise as serpents and innocent as doves'.

The call to be both faithful to truth, and to engage the world, is tremendously difficult and dangerous. There is no pre-packaged programme that will tell us all that we need to do. We need to let go of our dependency on methods, and instead lean on God's wisdom. We can however trust in this one fact, God has given us everything that we need.

His divine power has granted to us all things that pertain to life and godliness, through the knowledge of him who called us to his own glory and excellence. (2 Peter 1:3)

All Scripture is breathed out by God and profitable for teaching, for reproof, for correction, and for training in righteousness, that the man of God may be complete, equipped for every good work. (2 Timothy 3:16–17).

The more we know God's Word, the more we will know

God, and the more equipped we will be to stand in the storm and rescue the perishing.

The culture wants to redefine our faith—but our faith is built upon the revelation of God. God has revealed his ways through the Scriptures. As we root ourselves in the Word of God—especially those areas that the culture wants to destroy—we will bear the fruits of faithfulness. As we faithfully hold fast to God and his word, and as we faithfully seek to love and engage people—whilst resisting cultural conformity—we will emerge as a radical counter-cultural community. Our aim is not to be radical—our aim is to be faithful—but in today's context to be faithful is to be radical. And to be radical is to be unpopular. Consequently, we must always remember, as Christians, we should be more concerned with the approval of God, than acceptance with the world. We do the world no favours when we embrace their worldview. On the contrary, when we go against the flow, we are a greater blessing to the world because we function as the church should—as a lighthouse—not a dimmer switch.

Chapter One: Radical God

'God is dead.' No, not quite. But you could say, in the UK, 'God' is dying.[1] According to the polls only 38% of Britons believe in God.[2] Despite claims from the Prime Minister that Britain is still a Christian nation,[3] the decline in church attendance and the shifting cultural values suggests that Britain is in fact 'one of the most irreligious nations on the face of the earth.'[4] A recent survey carried out in Scotland reveals a similar picture, 70% of Scots say that they are just not interested in religion; 27% have a negative impression of Christianity; and only 8% say that faith in Jesus has 'deeply transformed their life'.[5] 'God' might not be dead, but to the majority of people he might as well be. Yet although God has been pushed to the margins of our culture; the Bible depicts God as being at the beginning, the centre, and the end of all human history and civilization. Unashamedly the Bible opens with the words: 'In the beginning, God created the heavens and the earth.' (Genesis 1:1)

Cultural climate

The opening words of Genesis in today's society generally meets with three types of responses—the concept of a creator God is either viewed as pathetically irrelevant, incredibly naïve, or oppressively insane. Consequently, the church is either ignored as insignificant, looked upon with patronizing mockery, or treated with aggressive hostility. We see the latter two responses combined in the statements of Professor Richard Dawkins. Dawkins, on BBC Radio's 'Thought for the Day' likened belief in a creator to humanity's 'crybaby phase'. The idea that the universe was created by God, according to Dawkins is nothing more than an 'infantile explanation'. In other words, belief in God is childlike and naïve and adults should know better. To believe in God in the 21st century is as ridiculous as adults believing in Santa Claus or the Tooth Fairy.[6]

Not content with patronizing mockery, Dawkins is also well known for his aggressive hostility. Religion, in Dawkins' mind is not just superstition which needs to be pitied, it's a disease that needs to be cured:

> It is fashionable to wax apocalyptic about the threat to humanity posed by the AIDS virus, 'mad cow' disease and many others, but I think that a case can be made that faith is one of the world's great evils, comparable to the smallpox virus but harder to eradicate.[7]

There you have it, according to the Doctor's diagnosis— faith is not only delusional, it's deadly! But what medicine does the doc prescribe in order to cure this deadly virus?

Dawkins instructs enlightened atheists to respond to religious people with insults and verbal abuse: 'Mock them. Ridicule them in public. Don't fall for the convention that we're all too polite to talk about religion.'[8] And Dawkins' disciples are only too happy to comply. We only need to look at the comments section on any news article which touches on matters to do with faith and religion and you will find the faithful followers of Dawkins launching their verbal attacks against all and any who would dare to bring God into the public sphere.

Just this week, as I write this, news spread that boxer Nick Blackwell had awoken from his coma after suffering a severe head injury in a fight with Chris Eubank Junior. The boxing world waited anxiously, hoping for the recovery of the young fighter. When news spread that he had recovered, boxing trainer Peter Fury tweeted, 'Great news Nick Blackwell has made full recovery. Mick said he's smiling & talking even telling jokes. In God we trust!!' No sooner had the announcement been made than the aggressive atheists were out in force. One commentator responding by saying,

> God has nothing to do with it ... those morons thanking god have no idea of the hard work and dedication of those doctors and nurses looking after him. Quite frankly to thank god for something he had nothing to do with is offensive.

Having expressed disgust, the atheistic evangelist reinforced her attack by referring to 'God' as 'an invisible non-existent bedtime story.'[9]

As is often the case, the thread escalated into a social

media cesspit. Instead of the focus being on the boxer's recovery, the thread became an atheistic battleground, all because a boxing trainer dared to bring God into the public sphere. We live in a context where even a public acknowledgement of God's providence results in a tirade of insults and abuse.

One of the more sinister and serious accusations to fly from the aggressive secularist's bow is the idea that children growing up in a religious household are victims of oppression. Dawkins has argued that Christian parents who teach their children to believe their faith are guilty of 'child abuse'.[10] In his mind, religious instruction in the home is an evil indoctrination that violates the rights of the child. Instead, they should be taught that religious thinking exists, but that 'scorn should be poured on its claims.'

Ironically, Dawkins himself is actually encouraging a form of indoctrination. Having worked with thousands of young people for over 15 years, I have encountered many young people who have been brought up to scorn religion, but they have not been brought up to think critically. All they have been fed is anti-religious dogma. When presented with an alternative perspective, very often the only weapons they have at their disposal are hostile insults.

Religion has fast become an increasingly censored area within the public spheres. The current conflict between equality legislation and religious freedom, and the multi-cultural tensions arising from terrorism, is increasingly leading to a situation where there is a major clamp-down on religious expression. God-talk seems to be the new social taboo.

One of the growing fears is the increase of radicalization. Because of Islamic religious extremism, there is an increasing fear surrounding religious instruction. In order for governments to deal with this, there seems to be a new tendency to treat all religious belief as suspect. Instead of differentiating between extreme Islamist ideology, and historic Christianity, both are often being placed in the same category. Take for example the following definition of a 'radicalizer', which is taken from a government document which has been designed to educate parents and teachers about the dangers of radical extremism. According to the document, a Radicalizer is 'an individual who encourages others to develop or adopt beliefs.'[11] Seriously. That's it. According to this definition, every Christian grand-parent, every Sunday-school teacher, every minister—and arguably, every Christian who seeks to share their faith with others, is a radicalizer.

This why there is something of an emerging totalitarian control over Christian education, and public expressions of faith in the workplace. Again, just this week there is a news article about an NHS employee whose appeal against accusations of 'bullying and harassment' have been denied.[12] The employee was disciplined for offering to pray for a fellow colleague, giving her a book, and inviting her to church. The Christian woman claimed that her colleague had been open and responsive, and their conversations were in the context of friendship and trust. Obviously not. Whatever the exact details of the case may be, the official response is sending a clear message home—Christians who seek to be open about their faith in the work-place face the risk of discipline.

The clampdown on religious instruction is further seen in government announcements to monitor all faith communities who educate children in the faith.[13] The new legislation is an attempt to tackle extremism, and Sunday Schools are included along with madrasas. The government's justification for monitoring Sunday School's is simply, 'We've got to do this in an even-handed way.' It's official, teaching children the basics of the Christian faith, (despite the fact we have been assured that we are still a Christian nation) has the potential to fall under the category of extremism and radicalization. Now, perhaps I'm not helping this perspective by calling this book 'Radical church' but this is the new reality, Biblical Christianity is officially radical—and the claims of Genesis Chapter One are some of the most radical claims in our faith, 'In the beginning, God created the heavens and the earth.' (Genesis 1:1)

Controversial Creator

Why is the claim that there is a God who created everything so radical and controversial? Quite simply, aggressive secularists think that the case for God is closed. It's a no brainer as far as they are concerned. If there were a God, there would be some kind of 'proof'. The accusations that faith in a creator God is naïve, delusional and dangerous, draw their strength from the idea that science has demolished God. The aggressive atheist campaign has been working hard to promote the idea that science and Christianity are at odds and that belief in God is unreasonable. Ultimately it boils down to a claim that to believe in God is to commit intellectual suicide. Again, this is used as ammunition against parents teaching their children to believe in God. If, as it is argued, to believe in God is to believe against all evidence to the contrary, then teaching children about God is to hinder their intellectual and personal development. To teach children that God created the world is the modern day equivalent of teaching them that the world is flat. We should know better.

Consequences of the Cultural Climate

The current anti-religious cultural climate creates a number of consequences for people in the church and people outside the church. For those who are in the church it creates a spirit of timidity. Christians are increasingly becoming self-conscious about their faith. Many are afraid to be open about what they believe, and fear talking about their faith lest they commit social suicide. It's understandable, society has become a cultural landmine. You never know who you are going to offend, who is going to report you, or how people will interpret what you say. Consequently, many believers are living dual lives. They have their private life which involves faith, and they have their public life which involves turning up on time, doing a good job and toeing the party line. In many ways we have become living characters in an Orwellian dystopia.

For those outside the church, the cultural climate creates a sense of security. With God out of the picture each person is free to live their own life in their own way, *If the experts have declared the death of God, who am I to disagree?* The claim that science has buried God means we can put to bed any niggling questions about the purpose of life, the day of Judgement and all that nasty stuff about heaven and hell—we now know that those were just old myths made up to scare the uneducated masses. Likewise the new equality legislation reinforces a sense of moral righteousness. The 'bad' people in society are those who cause division on the basis of belief. Religion has caused nothing but wars. Religion judges people and discriminates against people of different sexualities, so we tell ourselves, *I'm one of the good guys, I accept everyone for who they are—all that religion stuff is just negative, divisive and judgemental—we are better people without it.* A recent evangelism conference I attended called these issues 'defeater beliefs'. They are beliefs that people hold which prevent them from listening to the gospel.

Responding to the challenges

How can Christians respond to the current cultural challenges? How can we be confident in the existence of God when there are many voices confidently declaring that science has delivered to God the knock-out blow? What should we do about the fact that the public sphere is fast becoming a 'No God Zone'?[14] How should we respond to the criticisms that teaching our children to trust the Word of God is a form of oppression and child abuse? If we buckle and simply accept the status quo, we have ignored the clear command of Scripture which tells us, 'Do not be conformed to this world, but be transformed by the renewal of your mind, that by testing you may discern what is the will of God, what is good and acceptable and perfect' (Romans 12:2). If we allow the prevailing worldviews to shape our minds and hearts, we will be conformed into the image of the values of this world. If on the other hand, we allow our minds and our hearts to be moulded by the Word of God, we will be transformed and empowered to stand fast against the cultural conditioning.

But how do we do this in our current context? The Bible again is our key. Firstly, we need to be depending on the truth ourselves, secondly we need to declare the truth (and regularly have the truth declared to us), and thirdly we need to be prepared to discuss and debate the truth with those who do not believe.

Chapter Two: Radical Response

Before we can declare the truth to others, we need to *know* the truth for ourselves. Our culture is full of Christianized atheists; people who refer to themselves as 'Christian' but who don't have genuine saving faith in God. The Bible makes it clear that true faith is not simply giving some kind of mental assent that there is a God. The apostle James challenged this kind of thinking when he said, 'You believe that God is one; you do well. Even the demons believe— and shudder! (James 2:19).'

According to latest statistics, 52% of people in Scotland do not consider themselves 'religious'.[1] But what about the 48% who do? It is not identifying with a religion, or simply 'believing in God' that makes a person a Christian. A person who is a Christian is not simply a person who knows and accepts information *about* God; a Christian is a person who *knows* God. Jesus gave us the true definition of biblical faith when he said, 'And this is eternal life, that they know you the only true God, and Jesus Christ whom you have sent.' (John 17:3) As we can see from the Words of Jesus, true faith in God is incredibly important. A person with true faith has eternal life, a person without true faith hasn't. True faith is to *know* God, and to *know* Jesus Christ. In other words there is a level of assurance that accompanies true faith in God. We see this further illustrated in one of the clearest definitions of faith found in the New Testament.

> Now faith is the assurance of things hoped for, the conviction of things not seen. For by it the people of old received their commendation. By faith we understand that the universe was created by the word of God, so that what is seen was not made out of things that are visible. (Hebrews 11:1–3)

Once again we see that faith is closely associated with assurance. Faith is not simply the assent of the mind; it is also the assurance of the heart, and the yielding of the will. We embrace the truth of God with our mind, we receive the Spirit of God in our hearts, and we yield our wills in obedience to God. In other words, true faith involves trust, assurance and action. We call on God, we talk to God, we listen to God through his Word, and we seek to obey God. This is what the Bible talks about when it speaks of the fear of God: The friendship of the LORD is for those who fear him, and he makes known to them his covenant. (Psalm 25:14)

Those who know God, fear God. This is not a destructive fear, but a healthy fear. It's like the fear mingled with awe and adoration that grips a person when they see something incredible in creation. It's like awe that envelops a person as they gaze up at the starry sky at night and get a glimpse of how small they are in comparison to the vast universe. Whilst it is right to fear God, God in his amazing grace calls us into an intimate knowledge of himself. He calls us into friendship. A true Christian does not just have a religion with a creator; a true Christian has a relationship with a Father God.

It is this true knowledge of God that will enable us to withstand the increasing cultural pressures. As we said at the start, the biblical response to the cultural challenges is to be faithful to truth and engage the culture. The only way we will be able to do this is if we are personally depending on the truth of God. A genuine knowledge of God is the only foundation that will enable us to stand faithful and engage the culture.

Declare the truth

The Bible doesn't *suggest* the existence of God, it declares it. So must we. God is a preacher and the whole of creation is his pulpit: 'The heavens declare the glory of God, and the sky above proclaims his handiwork.' (Psalm 19:1) The Bible doesn't attempt to persuade people of God's existence it simply proclaims his existence. To the secularist, this is insanity. Why should anyone accept something so incredible on the authority of a book? Well, the answer to that question is that the authority of any book depends upon the credibility of the author—the Bible comes to us, not as the mere words of men, (although they were the instruments in penning it), it comes to us as the very Words of God.

Truth carries with it a sense of conviction, authenticity, and authority, and this is exactly what the Word of God conveys. Likewise, when God's Word is proclaimed, declared and spoken, the words carry a power, life and energy of their own. Consequently, God does not command his people to speculate about his existence, he commands his people to declare his existence. The Bible is full of exhortations for God's people to declare and proclaim, not only the existence—but the majesty and glory of God.

Declare his glory among the nations, his marvelous works among all the peoples! (Psalm 96:3)

I proclaim your might to another generation, your power to all those to come. (Psalm 71:18)

I will open my mouth in a parable; I will utter dark sayings from of old, which we have heard and known, And our fathers have told us. We will not hide them from their children, but tell to the coming generation the glorious deeds of the LORD, and his might, and the wonders that he has done. (Psalm 78:1–3)

I have told the glad news of deliverance in the great congregation; behold, I have not restrained my lips, as you know, O LORD. (Psalm 40:9)

But you are a chosen race, a royal priesthood, a holy nation, a people for his own possession, that you may proclaim the excellencies of him who called you out of darkness into his marvelous light. (2 Peter 2:9)

The Bible is absolutely clear; one of the primary callings

of God's people is to proclaim the wonder, works and ways of God. Notice who we are to declare God's Word to and where we are to declare God's Word. We are to declare God's Word 'among the nations'; to the next 'generation' and in the 'great congregation'. In other words, there is no sphere of life where God's Word should not be proclaimed. God's Word is to be proclaimed in the church to his people; in the home to our family, and in the marketplace to unbelievers.

One of the greatest failings within the church in recent times has been the loss of anointed, biblical, *Big-God* preaching. The secular context has led many churches to develop a complex which has resulted in a cultural rebrand which is designed to make church more attractive. On the one hand this is good, some churches really do need to be kicked into the 21st century, but the rebranding has also embraced many of the culture's weaknesses. In an attempt to be more relevant, many churches have lost their prophetic edge. Instead of calling people from darkness to light, we are inviting people to come and sit in the dark. Instead of expository preaching, we are delivering talks on how to have a better lifestyle. Instead of preaching the greatness of God, we are delivering motivational speeches on the greatness of human potential. We are no longer hearing the call to repentance, instead we are being told,— 'everyone's a winner' and rather than beholding the Glory of God, we are invited to discover the Champion in YOU!

The only way to counter the influence of humanistic thinking that shapes our society and has infiltrated the church is to return to God-centred preaching. As the church we don't just declare that there is a God, we also declare who this God is. It's time to stop viewing God through the lens of humanism, and instead view humanism through the lens of God. Just who is this God that we are speaking about? Isaiah, declares him to us:

Go on up to a high mountain,
O Zion, herald of good news;
lift up your voice with strength,
O Jerusalem, herald of good news;
lift it up, fear not;
say to the cities of Judah,
'Behold your God!'
10 Behold, the Lord God comes with might,
and his arm rules for him;
behold, his reward is with him,
and his recompense before him.
11 He will tend his flock like a shepherd;
he will gather the lambs in his arms;
he will carry them in his bosom,
and gently lead those that are with young.

12 Who has measured the waters in the hollow of his hand
and marked off the heavens with a span,
enclosed the dust of the earth in a measure
and weighed the mountains in scales
and the hills in a balance?
13 Who has measured the Spirit of the Lord,
or what man shows him his counsel?
14 Whom did he consult,
and who made him understand?
Who taught him the path of justice,

and taught him knowledge,
and showed him the way of understanding?
15 Behold, the nations are like a drop from a bucket,
and are accounted as the dust on the scales;
behold, he takes up the coastlands like fine dust. (Isaiah
40:9–15)

If we take seriously the call to declare the whole counsel of God in our churches, we will immediately find ourselves being counter-cultural. The culture is influenced by post-modern thinking. Post-modern thinking is relativistic, non-authoritative and relational. Consequently, Post-moderns don't want declarations, they want dialogue; they prefer ambiguity instead of certainty; and they want informality, not authority. Where the church capitulates to the postmodern agenda, there you will find a church with no voice. A church with no voice is a church that has abandoned its calling. The church is a prophetic community that is commissioned to declare, 'Thus sayeth the Lord.'

Declaring does not always mean 'preaching', but it does include preaching. How we declare the truth of God will vary depending on the circumstances. Declaring the truth of God in the home will look different to how it looks from the pulpit on a Sunday morning. Likewise, declaring truth 'among the nations' in the market place does not mean jumping on a soap box and shouting at people. Whilst I do think that there is still a place for street preaching, it is not the way that most Christians will communicate their faith in the market place. For most of us, 'declaring' the Word of God will simply take the form of truth-telling, in other words, speaking openly and honestly about the Word of God as the occasion and opportunities arise. At the very least, when questioned about our faith, all true Christians should be able to share their testimony, and explain their reasons for trusting in Christ as their Lord and Saviour. Our default condition as Christians should be that of 'always being prepared to make a defence to anyone who asks you for a reason for the hope that is in you; yet do it with gentleness and respect.' (2 Peter 3:15)

Discuss and debate

Sociologists say we live in a post-Christian culture; however, with the emergence of secularism, there is a generation of young people who are growing up in families with no knowledge of the Christian faith. Arguably some of the people we encounter will not be post-Christian in their attitude, but pre-Christian. Determining where people are at is essential if we are going to have any meaningful conversation. We can't assume that people understand the Christian terminology. There is no point in just telling people they 'need to believe in God' or they 'need to get saved' without explaining who God is and what it means to be saved.

I once asked several groups of teenagers what they understand by the word 'God'—the answers were amazing. Some when they thought of God thought of 'Clouds', others said, 'an old man with a beard, in the Sky'. Others had a concept of 'light', and others thought of an 'old church building' or a 'Religious Education class' (the reason for the latter was that in this young person's life, RE was the only place where God was ever mentioned). We can't take anything for granted today. Before we can instruct people about the Bible, we will likely have to deconstruct some of the faulty concepts they already have.

Generally speaking, I tend to find that there are three main attitudes towards Christianity prevalent in our culture today. The majority of people are simply indifferent to the claims of Christianity. The concept of God holds zero interest or relevance to them. They find the subject boring, and switch off immediately as soon as the topic arises. The next group of people are antagonistic. The Christian faith makes them angry. As soon as the topic comes up they are ready to get into a skirmish. This second group is growing. The third group is a minority, but they are people who are interested in spiritual matters. They are open to exploring issues such as the meaning of life, the existence of God and life after death. Understanding where a person is coming from should influence how we respond to them. We need to awaken the complacent; challenge the antagonist; and lead the seeker to Christ.

One of the encouraging outcomes of the death of Christendom is the fact that we find ourselves in a context that has more in common with the early church. Consequently we can learn lessons from how the apostles engaged with the various cultures they encountered in their own missional endeavours. If we look at Paul's example we can see that his approach involved both declaration and discussion. He declared the truth about the resurrection, but he also reasoned and conversed with people.

Now while Paul was waiting for them at Athens, his spirit was provoked within him as he saw that the city was full of idols. So he reasoned in the synagogue with the Jews and the devout persons, and in the market-place every day with those who happened to be there. Some of the Epicurean and Stoic philosophers also conversed with him. And some said, 'What does this babbler wish to say?' Others said, 'He seems to be a preacher of foreign divinities'—because he was preaching Jesus and the resurrection. (Acts 17:16–18)

Paul wasn't afraid to engage with the prevalent worldviews of his day. In our own day, the New Atheism is a movement that is increasing and gaining some momentum. Dawkins has sparked a fire of controversy and it continues to spread. Most people in society aren't schooled in philosophy or the academic works of the New Atheists, yet many people have adopted the slogans of the new movement. Many people presume that science and religion are at war, or that science has proven there is no God. As the church we need to engage this mind-set and show it up for what it is—a myth.

If science and theism (belief in God) were incompatible, then it would be the case that there would be no scientists who are theists. In reality, there were two surveys carried out, the first in 1916 and the second 1996 both of which demonstrate that approximately 40% of Scientists are theists. Despite the hostility that often surrounds the science and faith discussion, many scientists have spoken out about the compatibility of faith and science. The botanist professor, Sir Ghillean Prance, states: 'For many years I have believed that God is the great designer behind all nature ... All my studies in science since then have confirmed my faith.'

Likewise, a number of people have the idea in their head that the theory of the Big Bang has somehow rendered God out of a job. The reality is that one of the key figures who helped establish the Big Bang theory was a theist. Nobel Prize winner, Arno Penzias, when interviewed about the impact of the Big bang theory upon his faith, said: 'The best data we have are exactly what I would have predicted, had I had nothing to go on but the five books of Moses, the Psalms, the Bible as a whole.'

In other words, the impact of the scientific evidence upon Arno, as a theist, was not to throw his hands up in the air in despair, abandon his faith, and head down to the pub—on the contrary the evidence confirmed the teaching of the Bible. The scientific evidence confirms that there once was nothing, and then there was something. The Big Bang theory simply confirms that the universe had a starting point, and this is exactly what the Bible teaches, 'In the beginning, God created the heavens and the earth.' (Genesis 1:1). Contrary to popular opinion, science does not teach us why the world started. At best it can help us understand how some of creation ticks, but it does not in any way explain away the need for a creator. If anything, the more one looks at the scientific evidence, the more one sees the fine tuning of the universe, and the more one sees the hand of God.

Creating opportunities to discuss the claims of Christianity can have a positive effect on the church-goer and the non-church goer. For the non-church goer it can create an environment where they are safe to explore the faith in a non-threatening environment; for the churchgoer, it can be an opportunity to deepen their faith. I discovered this a few years ago when I was leading a Bible study at a church. We were exploring the question of why people continue to come to church yet hold back from professing faith in Christ. The outcome of this discussion was a real learning curve for me. I'd presumed that one of the main reasons holding people back from professing faith was simply a lack of assurance of salvation. What I discovered is that some people in the pew are not even convinced there is a God.

'I'd be a hypocrite to profess faith' said a member of the group, who had been attending church his whole life—over 60 years.

'Why?' I asked.

'Well, I'm not even sure I believe—I mean, do you have to suspend the scientific evidence, in order to believe?'

I hadn't expected that. Here was a man who had attended church all his life whilst in his heart he was wrestling with the relationship between God and science. The church had clearly failed in two areas here. It had failed because it obviously was not addressing the issues of the day in the preaching, but it had also failed because it had not created an environment for these issues to be explored and discussed.

I decided to host some science versus God events. I ran them in the local community hall in order to attract people who may not feel comfortable coming into a church building. When it came round to the night of the event, only three people from outside the church attended, all three of them were atheists and two of them held a PhD in Biology. One of them arrived with a folder full of notes and quotes at the ready in order to demolish the arguments for the existence of God. At the end of it, we were not able to persuade the atheists to change their position, but we were able to demonstrate warm-heartedness and a willingness to engage openly and respectfully with them. This seemed to have more impact than the arguments. However, the arguments did have a positive effect on our man in the pew. The outcome of participating in the event, listening to the debate between myself and the atheists, and following up the sessions with some apologetics literature, was that he was able to say, 'I can now see there is convincing evidence for the existence of God.'

When I decided to host the *Science versus God* event, I advertised it on a local social media group. The abuse I received was astounding. I was told that Christians should not be advertising their events in public spaces (when did Christians have their citizenship revoked?) and I was mocked and insulted by people I have never met. However, the more people commented, and the more the accusations escalated, the more free publicity the event received. By God's grace, I kept my cool, refrained from getting into a social media troll fest, and responded with gentleness and calmness (not my natural disposition). And whilst the event did not lead to any conversions, it did persuade me that discussion-based evangelism is an essential tool that the church can use to equip its members and engage with unbelievers. It's risky, but it's worth it.

Christianity is Controversial

Ultimately, belief in God is an increasingly controversial issue. If we are to be the people of God, we too, by default, will be controversial. There is no escaping that. We need to know and understand our times, we need to know and understand God, and we need to bridge the gap between the church and the culture. As we seek to be a faithful people, trusting and proclaiming our faithful God, we will be perceived as a radical people with a radical God. But let us remember the words of Daniel, 'the people who know their God shall stand firm and take action.'(Daniel 11:32).

Chapter Three: Radical Reformation

The Reformation was a time of great shaking and awakening for the church. Prior to the Reformation, the church was a mess. Instead of transforming the world, the church had become conformed to the world. Instead of being known for truth, humility and love; the church was marked by deception, exploitation and corruption. Many church leaders were shepherds who fed themselves at the expense of the sheep. The masses of people were 'harassed and helpless, like sheep without a shepherd.' (Matthew 9:36). However, all of this would change after Martin Luther nailed his 95 theses to the church door at Wittenberg on October 31, 1517. Luther's boldness proved to be a prophetic act that would ultimately spark the fires of Reformation and revival. He was challenging the established church of the day by calling her to examine her beliefs and practices in the light of Scripture alone. Luther's emphasis on the Word of God brought him into direct conflict with the courts of the Church. Only four years later in 1521 at Worms, Luther would be pressurized to withdraw and renounce his teaching. Luther's response was cataclysmic.

> Unless I am convinced by the testimony of the Scriptures or by clear reason, for I do not trust either in the pope or in councils alone, since it is well known that they often err and contradict themselves, I am bound to the Scriptures I have quoted and my conscience is captive to the Word of God. I cannot and I will not retract anything, since it is neither safe nor right to go against conscience. I cannot do otherwise. Here I stand. May God help me. Amen.

Luther's stand led to Scripture being wrestled free from the chains of traditionalism and superstition; the Reformation was about the Word of God being restored to its rightful place within the church. A Bible freed from the control of the church, led to a church free from the traditions of men. The church transitioned from being an oppressive institution that enslaved people, to being a missional force that freed people. The gospel rang forth with clarity and power once again. The man-centred church gave way to a Christ-centred church, and the church stopped exploiting the poor and rediscovered its call to empower the poor.

The Reformation was not perfect. One of the greatest tragedies of the Reformation has been the splintering of the church. Since the time of the Reformation, many denominations and divisions have emerged. The unity of the church has been greatly hindered in many different ways. However, the protestant, reformed, and evangelical churches—despite having many differences, historically have held significant truths in common. The centrality, authority and sufficiency of Scripture are examples of some of these core truths. When Luther said, 'Unless I am convinced by the testimony of the Scriptures ... I am bound to the Scriptures ... my conscience is captive to the Word of God.' He was paving the way for *Sola Scriptura* (Scripture Alone) to become the foundational doctrine of the Reformation. Indeed it was Luther's commitment to *Sola Scriptura* that brought him into sharp conflict with the Roman Catholic Church. As the Reformation evolved and developed, *Sola Scriptura* became the bench mark for the reformed churches. The commitment to *Sola Scriptura* can clearly be seen in the writings of the reformers and the various reformed confessions.

Why was Scripture given such a preeminent place within the reformed churches? Firstly, it is through the Scriptures that we come to know God. Whilst God reveals his existence through his creation, creation does not explicitly reveal the way of salvation. The reformed believe that God has two books, the first one being the book of nature, and the second one being the written Word of God. Through the Scriptures God has chosen to make himself known, and has invited us to come to know him. The Belgic Confession says God 'makes himself known to us more openly by his holy and divine Word, as much as we need in this life, for his glory and for the salvation of his own.'[1] In other words all that is needed for knowing and obeying God is to be found within the Scriptures.

Consequently, the Reformation distinguished between the written words of men, and the written Word of God. It differentiated between the uninspired spoken words of pastors, popes and councils, and the inspired Word of God. Again the Belgic confessions states: 'We confess that this Word of God was not sent nor delivered by the will of men, but that holy men of God spoke, being moved by the Holy Spirit.' These were not just clever ideas about the Bible that were formulated by men; these confessions were designed to be a summary of the Bible's own teaching about the Word of God. The Bible is not the Word of God because men say so, on the contrary, people should embrace the Scriptures as the Word of God because the Scriptures say so. It is God's testimony that counts.

To believe in *Sola Scriptura* is to believe in the authority and sufficiency of Scripture. It is to accept that the Word of God is the final authority on all matters of faith and practice, and it is to trust that the Scriptures are sufficient. That is, God has given us everything we need in the Scriptures to save us, sanctify us and to equip us for service. Again, the reformed confessions stressed these central truths:

We include in the Holy Scripture the two volumes of the Old and New Testaments. They are canonical books with which there can be no quarrel at all ... We receive all these books and these only as holy and canonical, for the regulating, founding, and establishing of our faith. And we believe without a doubt all things contained in them—not so much because the church receives and approves them as such but above all because the Holy Spirit testifies in our hearts that they are from God, and also because they prove themselves to be from God. For even the blind themselves are able to see that the things predicted in them do happen

...We believe that this Holy Scripture contains the will of God completely and that everything one must believe to be saved is sufficiently taught in it ... Therefore we must not consider human writings—no matter how holy their authors may have been—equal to the divine writings; nor may we put custom, nor the majority, nor age, nor the passage of time or persons, nor councils, decrees, or official decisions above the truth of God, for truth is above everything else.[2]

Historical Evangelicalism

The churches which have sprung from the reformation have historically been grouped together under the banner of 'evangelicalism'. However, before we go any further, it is important to clarify what we mean by evangelicalism. We live in a context where many Christians have no interest in labels—labels are considered to be too divisive, instead, it is argued, we should focus on the fact that we are all brothers and sisters in Christ. Defining evangelicalism is also difficult, not only because many people have no patience for terms and theological adjectives—but also because the word 'evangelical' (like many other theological terms) has lost its meaning. However, historically evangelicals have been marked by core commitments. Again not all evangelicals are agreed on what these defining marks are, some have settled for a minimalist framework,[3] whereas others have argued for the need for a more detailed definition.[4]

Whilst the evangelical churches which sprung from the reformed churches have not always had the same emphasis on detailed creeds, they were united by their commitment to the principle of Sola Scriptura. Church historian, David Bebbington has argued that one of the defining marks[5] of historic evangelicalism[6] is, 'Biblicism: a high regard for and obedience to the Bible as the ultimate authority.'[7] In other words, evangelicalism was a historical product of the Reformation. If we study the early evangelicals we will easily identify the spirit of the Reformation—an uncompromising zeal and commitment to the authority and sufficiency of Scripture.

Evangelicalism Today

Today, there has been a clear departure from core evangelical and reformed convictions in many of the churches that trace their roots back to the Reformation and evangelical movements. *Sola Scriptura* is no longer, in practice, the defining doctrine in many post-Reformation churches. As we have seen, Luther, the reformed confessions, and evangelical historians have understood the importance of the authority of the Bible, but this is rarely how evangelicals describe their relationship to Scripture today. In answering the question, 'What is an Evangelical?' the Evangelical Alliance says, 'We're evangelical. We're passionate: about God, about the Church and about the Bible.'[8] On the surface that looks good, but it's one thing to say we are passionate about the Bible, it's another thing to state clearly what we believe about the Bible. This is one of the great weaknesses of the contemporary church; we're more concerned with being passionate than articulate. But when it comes to Christianity, we substitute being articulate for being passionate, at our peril. The reformers were passionate too—and their passion changed the face of nations—but they were passionately articulate, and it was this clear, articulate and passionate commitment to *Sola Scriptura* that led to cultural confrontation and Reformation.

Contemporary evangelicals wax lyrical about passion and transformation, but they will never see the transformation they desire until they recover a deep conviction about the authority and sufficiency of Scripture. When you really say that the Bible is the Word of God, you are saying that the Bible is the final authority. When you apply the Bible to life, you are saying 'Thus sayeth the Lord'. Consequently, when you say the Bible is the authoritative word on a particular matter, you are dethroning all other pretenders. You are not only proclaiming, you are also protesting. To truly stand on *Sola Scriptura* is to speak into the culture on the grounds of scriptural authority, and that will immediately bring you into conflict with the competing ideologies and world views of the day. When the church speaks with the voice of *Sola Scriptura*, it speaks prophetically, and it challenges the wisdom of the social elites, political correctness and the social trends of the masses. Put another way, if Martin Luther had simply said, 'I'm passionate about the Bible' there never would have been a Reformation. The Church courts would have said, 'We are too.' And that would have been the end of it. But thank God he wasn't just passionate about the Bible, but his conscience was captive to the Bible—and that changed everything.

Whilst most contemporary evangelicals still claim to have a high view of Scripture, the reality is they have lost their grip on the authority of Scripture. Many Christians, and leaders, who are part of the contemporary evangelical movement, are not only neglecting the centrality of Scripture, they are unware of their own historical roots. It's almost as if modern evangelicals were kidnapped at birth, and raised by different parents. And when they are eventually introduced to their biological parents, they are incredibly disappointed. They don't see the family resemblance, they don't like the family name, and they can't stand the family history and heritage. Many contemporary Christians don't understand how all that confessional stuff about *Sola Scriptura* has anything to do with their 'awesome relationship with Jesus' (it's all a bit heavy) but they fail to understand if it weren't for the Reformation, and the reformers' commitment to *Sola Scriptura*, they would never have known they could have a relationship with Jesus!

Cultural trends

Recent research amongst those who consider themselves 'practicing Christians' in Scotland reveals that less than 50% of Christians hold to the doctrine of *Sola Scriptura*.

1. 12% say the Bible is the actual Word of God and should be taken literally, word for word.

2. 37% say the Bible is the inspired Word of God and has no errors, although some verses are meant to be symbolic rather than literal.

3. 34% say the Bible is the inspired Word of God but has some factual or historical errors.

4. 12% say the Bible was not inspired by God but tells how the writers of the Bible understood the ways and principles of God.[9]

Taking into account the clumsy definitions of option one and two, and also the fact that option two probably includes a proportion of people who believe in *Sola Scriptura* (if not all of them)—it is clear that it is a minority of people who consider themselves Christians who hold to *Sola Scriptura*.

The post-reformation church situation is a confusing and complex scenario. The Scottish survey revealed that 69% percent of self-identifying Christians were simply cultural Christians and only 5% identified themselves as being evangelical. Ironically 26% claimed to be 'non-evangelical born again'. This is fascinating because historically, Christians who claimed to be 'born-again Christians' were, by definition, evangelicals. In the survey, those who identify themselves as born-again non-evangelicals, are Christians who claim to have a personal relationship with Jesus as their Saviour, but do not hold to the classical characteristics of an evangelical as set forth in the Bebbington criteria. We looked at one of the criteria earlier, but now we shall now look at all four factors.

Bebbington identifies the core marks of evangelicalism as:

1. Conversionism: the belief that lives need to be transformed through a 'born-again' experience and a lifelong process of following Jesus;

2. Activism: the expression and demonstration of the gospel in missionary and social reform efforts;

3. Biblicism: a high regard for and obedience to the Bible as the ultimate authority and

4. Crucicentrism: a stress on the sacrifice of Jesus Christ on the cross as making possible the redemption of humanity.[10]

Those who identify as born again non-evangelical whilst embracing the first characteristic, are unable to accept all four characteristics. Given that even liberal Christians embrace a form of the second characteristic (Activism), it is safe to presume that the problematic characteristics for born-again non-evangelical Christians are the third and fourth characteristics—Biblicism and Crucicentrism. Amongst all the doctrines of Scripture, none have come more under attack in recent years than the doctrine of Scripture and the doctrine of the atonement.

These problems are not limited to Scotland or even the UK. The issues are similar across the pond. For example, one pastor in the US confesses that he was surprised to discover he has to spend more time defending the Bible against attacks from professing Christians than atheists.[11] Other US pastors have written extensively about these problems. Authors such as Gary Gilley (*This little Church went to Market: Is the modern church reaching out, or selling out?*); Michael Horton (*Christless Christianity: The Alternative Gospel of the American Church*); and James Montgomery Boice: (*Whatever Happened to the Gospel of Grace: Recovering the doctrines that shook the world*) all reveal the same problem, and the problem is this—evangelicals have abandoned their Biblical foundations. The outcome of this situation is the growing reality that there are a great number of people attending churches that have a reformation and evangelical heritage but are no longer evangelical. Call it post-evangelical, post-reformation or whatever—the bottom line is they stand in the tradition and heritage of evangelicalism, but they have lost their core identity as evangelicals. (For those who don't like labels, couldn't care less, and don't get what the big issue is—let me put it this way—this means there are an increasing number of Christians who have abandoned the Word of God). However, the really concerning issue is this, born-again *non-evangelicals* seem to be in the majority. And, it is my concern, that it is this kind of Christianity that defines and dominates some of the UK's (and the US's) most active, contemporary and large-scale churches.

To make it trickier, the problem of the contemporary born-again non-evangelical church culture is not limited to certain denominations. We are dealing with a cultural issue, not a denominational issue. Consequently, this new kind of church—churches full of people who claim to be born-again whilst at the same not holding to a Biblical view of Scripture or the atonement, are springing up all over the place. Some are new church plants, and others are old, mainline denominations who have rebranded their image to embrace the new-church look. Consequently, we have churches which on paper are still Presbyterian, Anglican, Baptist, Methodist, Brethren, Pentecostal, and on paper may even still subscribe to a Statement of faith which claims to hold to a Biblical position on the doctrine of Scripture; but in practice these churches have embraced certain cultural trends that have led to a serious downgrading of the doctrine of the atonement and the doctrine of Scripture.

How culture is shaping the church more than Scripture

Young evangelicals may still attend a church which holds to a Statement of Faith that believes in the Bible's divine inspiration, authority and sufficiency. Yet the reality is they spend most of their time in a culture which eats, breathes and sleeps a contrary worldview. Humanism is the accepted belief system of the western world. Humanism shapes our politics, our education system, our media and our understanding of rights and responsibilities.

Whilst not everyone would claim to be a humanist, the reality is all of us to varying degrees are shaped by humanistic values, attitudes and behaviours. I've taught Religion and Philosophy for seven years in Scottish schools, and even in a Highland context, where there is still a higher proportion of the population influenced by cultural Christianity, the majority of students identify more closely with a humanistic worldview than a Christian worldview. The clearest example of this is when we looked at a quiz which was developed by the British Humanist Society.[12] The quiz is designed to help participants discover how humanistic their beliefs were. I have used this quiz with hundreds of pupils over a period of several years. The results were the same each time. Whilst most of the students had never heard of humanism, and did not consider themselves humanist, they were surprised to discover that their worldview was in fact humanist. I would have no doubts that the results would be the same for most state schools in the UK.

How is this possible? How can people hold to a belief system that they have never even heard of? One of the reasons is simply down to the fact that our society has become increasingly secular. Let me use an analogy, in the next chapter, to illustrate this.

Chapter Four: Radical Reshaping

Once upon a time the UK and Christianity were married. Hand in hand the government and Christianity walked down through the centuries. The Christian faith shaped government laws and legislation. Legislation shaped education and media which in turn shaped and influenced culture and individuals. The UK was Christian. However, like many marriages—the relationship was not a harmonious one. In fact, it was quite turbulent. The government's love soon turned cold, and the loveless relationship soon led to a separation—not a divorce but a separation. However, when it comes to societies and worldviews, there is no such thing as a vacuum. When one belief system goes, another must take its place. So the government found a mistress. This new mistress is a lot more fun and less restrictive than the old wife. And so, the mistress now sits as the dominant force in shaping the UK's values, ethics and behaviours. It is now humanism which shapes government, which shapes legislation, education and media which then shapes the values and attitudes of individuals and culture. The UK and Christianity are not yet divorced, but the wife is certainly being frozen out. She's no longer welcome at the big events, her previous influence is being re-written, and her character is now being maligned. Many of her children—are not only waiting impatiently for news of the divorce—they can't wait to celebrate her funeral.

The divorce is not through. There are still remnants from the marriage. Christianity is still taught in Religious Education. In Scotland it still holds the greater proportion of the syllabus. We still have worship assembly, and in the main, these services will be delivered by local church ministers. Schools still have chaplains from local churches. Gideons International still have freedom to distribute Bibles to schools, hotels, hospitals and so on. But these freedoms are constantly coming under attack. There is a humanistic secular agenda to shut down these Christian activities. The separation is underway, but the divorce has not been finalized.

So, what does the influence of humanism have to do with our attitude to the Scriptures? To understand this, first we need to understand some core humanist beliefs. The British Humanist Society defines a humanist as someone who:

- trusts to the scientific method when it comes to understanding how the universe works and rejects the idea of the supernatural (and is therefore an atheist or agnostic).

- makes their ethical decisions based on reason,

empathy, and a concern for human beings and other sentient animals.

- believes that, in the absence of an afterlife and any discernible purpose to the universe, human beings can act to give their own lives meaning by seeking happiness in this life and helping others to do the same.[1]

These three basic principles of humanism should make it clear that humanism is the antithesis of the Christian faith. Humanism 'rejects the idea of the supernatural', yet Christians believe not only in a supernatural God, but a supernatural book. We believe in the inspiration of Scripture, that is, we believe that Scripture is 'God-breathed', 'All Scripture is breathed out by God and profitable for teaching, for reproof, for correction, and for training in righteousness.' (2 Timothy 3:16) The humanist rejects the moral authority of religious texts, and instead 'makes their ethical decisions based on reason'—in other words, we—not God—determine what is right and wrong. Finally, the humanist worldview has a naturalist outlook on the world, humanism denies the afterlife, and claims 'human beings can act to give their own lives meaning by seeking happiness in this life.' In other words, there is no eternity, there is no Day of Judgement—all we have is now, so live for the moment, seek happiness and try to be a jolly nice chap. Humanism limits our perspective to the here and now, the Bible broadens our perspective by linking the here and now to the ever-after. In other words, the Scriptures are given to make us conscious of eternity. The Westminster Confession says, 'The whole counsel of God concerning all things necessary for his own glory, man's salvation, faith and life, is either expressly set down in Scripture, or by good and necessary consequence may be deduced from Scripture.'[2] The Westminster Confession of Faith is making it clear that one of the primary purposes of Scripture is to reveal to us the way of salvation.

A passing glance at the contemporary church is enough to demonstrate that the church is shaped more by humanism than the Scriptures. The church has lost confidence in the supernatural power of the Word of God; consequently, expository preaching has been replaced with life talks. Instead of understanding that the Bible is given to equip us how to live in the light of eternity, many young evangelicals have been conned into thinking that the Bible is a spiritual self-help book that's designed to help us live our best life now. The real scandal in all of this is this, many evangelicals have no clue that humanism is eclipsing Christianity yet the secular press can see it for what it is. One headline sums it up perfectly when it describes 'The Great Evangelical Rebranding' and highlights the fact that 'US evangelicals no longer talk about how God will smite you. Now it's all about personal, spiritual and material fulfilment.'[3] It's not just America—this kind of pseudo-evangelicalism has become the standard diet in UK evangelical churches. It's no coincidence that the evangelical rebranding reflects the values of humanism—a down-grading of the importance of eternity, and an emphasis on enjoying the here and now, this is the outworking of humanism in the church. The church may not have abandoned God completely, but it has radically redefined itself in humanistic terms. Consequently, the

Bible, where it is still used, is often interpreted through a humanistic filter, and Bible verses are plucked from their context to promote humanistic values.

Further Cultural Challenges

There are several other cultural ideologies that dominate the wider culture and consequently influence and shape the church. Along with humanism, these ideologies have an impact on all of the major doctrines of the Christian faith, not least the doctrine of *Sola Scriptura*. Where these ideologies are dominant, a church's commitment to *Sola Scriptura* will be weak. What are these ideologies? They are relativism, pragmatism, experientialism and individualism.

Relativism

Relativism is the idea that there are no absolute truths—we all have varying perspectives, each of which are considered to be equally valid. The ideology of relativism assures us that 'everything is relative'—nothing is absolute. Like humanism, most folk may never have heard the word relativism, yet multitudes of people embrace a relativistic worldview. You can usually tell when someone is influenced by relativism, they will respond to truth claims with an indifferent, 'well, that's just your perspective'.

On the surface, relativism looks like a tolerant worldview—all truths are valid, everyone's viewpoint carries equal weight. In reality, it's very intolerant. Start speaking to a relativist in absolute terms and you will soon discover how intolerant relativists are. In reality, relativism is self-contradictory. The claim that there is no absolute truth, is in itself an absolute truth claim. So, relativists are tolerant of all other truth claims, providing those truth claims submit to the principle that they are simply *a* perspective, not *the* truth. If however, someone dares to say that a person, an idea, or a truth claim is wrong, the relativist will react in anger accusing the person of being intolerant, narrow-minded and arrogant. Certainty is the antithesis of relativism.

How does this affect the church's confidence in *Sola Scriptura*? To embrace *Sola Scriptura*, is to stand in the line of prophets and apostles and state, 'Thus sayeth the Lord'. Relativism has no room for 'Thus sayeth the Lord'. Consequently, when relativistic attitudes prevail in church contexts, there is no freedom for the Bible to speak with any level of authority or certainty. The church becomes a melting pot of opinions and ideologies and the Bible is silenced.

Can Scripture really be silenced in the church? Is relativism really a problem for the church in the West or the church in the UK? Absolutely. Just look at almost any issue of importance in the UK today and you will find the same thing—Christians without a clear, united and biblical voice. It is no better in evangelical circles, in fact—it is worse. At least the national churches are able to wheel out their leading churchmen to make a politically correct, non-offensive, but Bible-compromising sentiments but evangelicals are so disjointed they are unable to speak with unity, authority and certainty on almost any subject. This is a disgrace.

Pragmatism

Evangelicals were once known for the emphasis on

biblical proclamation, now they are known for cultural pragmatism. Pragmatism is an approach to life and ministry that operates on the principle, 'whatever works'. Pragmatism, in and of itself is not, bad but when pragmatism becomes the defining principle in our church life, leadership style and approach to ministry—we are in treacherous waters.

Church-growth philosophies have become so widespread, that pragmatism in many circles is the new orthodoxy. But there are consequences, when pragmatism becomes king, revelation gives way to innovation. Scripture—which is the primary means by which the church is to govern its life, be equipped for ministry, and engage in service—gets relegated to the shelf, and leadership gurus and principles take centre stage. Success becomes defined by numbers. The Bible no longer sets the pattern for church-life, instead churches are buying into models of ministry that are packaged and sold to us by the latest mega church strategist.

In the nine years I worked for an interdenominational youth organization, I observed this trend throughout various contemporary and denominational churches. On one occasion I observed this principle at a national and denominational level. I was invited to attend an 'emerging leaders' conference in Scotland. This conference was hosted by an evangelical denomination for the benefit of the various leaders within their churches across the nation. The conference was about raising up leaders, changing the church and connecting with culture. The conference may as well have been called, 'How to grow your church without prayer, the Bible and the Power of the Holy Spirit', because that's exactly what it was. It was a conference on how to better market the church, and that marketing explicitly involved the church moving away from being defined scripturally to being defined culturally.

Experientialism

The rise of charismatic Christianity has had an impact on almost every denomination. Many churches have embraced varying elements to varying degrees. Evangelicals are still divided over the charismatic question. Some see it as a renewing influence, others see it as degenerative influence. Some leading charismatics have highlighted that the movement is in crisis, and that many unbiblical practices have swept into the church through the charismatic movement.[4] In this regard, non-charismatic, and biblically-minded charismatic share the same concerns. One of the major problems which has accompanied the charismatic renewal is the emphasis on experience instead of Scripture.

Biblical Christianity is experiential—the new birth is an experience whereby the individual is brought into a life of communion with the triune God. However, one of the problems with many expressions of charismatic Christianity is the fact that experience has become central. In Christianity, Scripture, and not experience needs to be at the centre of our individual and church lives. The Scriptures are objective, experience is subjective. When we shift from truth-centred spirituality to experience-centred spirituality we exchange Biblical Christianity for mysticism.

There is a further problem with experience-centred

Christianity, it leads to liberalism. It leads to a Christianity that minimizes the central role of Scripture. Consequently, many evangelical charismatics have more in common with liberal Christians than conservative or reformed Christians. It's not that the latter deny experience, it's simply the fact that former elevate experience above Scripture. Increasingly evangelical charismatics and liberal Christians are using the same language. They talk about relationship instead of religion; they talk about the transforming love of God—and they are united in what they don't talk about—they don't talk about sin, repentance or the judgement to come—this is negative and does not fit with the positive experience they want people to experience. There are real issues here, charismatic Christianity is the fastest growing section of the church, but what kind of churches are being produced? The answer is, in many places, an increasingly relativistic church. A church which highly regards experience and individuality, but downplays Scripture and doctrine.

Individualism
Despite the fact that education, media, and government talk a lot about community, and communities, the western world is predominantly individualistic. Individualism is also the mark of modern evangelicalism. In one sense this is unavoidable, the gospel does come to us as individuals. Individually we will stand before God on the day of judgement. Individuals need to repent of their own sins, and trust in Jesus personally, if they are to have any hope of salvation. However, there is also a sinful individualism. The gospel is not only about individuals, it is about families, and it is about the church—God's redeemed community.

Whilst the church should meet the needs of individuals, it should never be defined by individualism. Yet this is exactly what has taken place.

Ever since the reformation there have always been independent churches, yet even many of these churches were careful to demonstrate that they were part of the historic church of Christ. However, what we are seeing in 21st century evangelicalism, is not just the rise of independent churches, but the rise of individualistic churches. Churches are springing up all over the place. Who are they and where do they come from? They are the product and vision of an individual leader. Many of these leaders will claim some sort of apostolic role or gifting, and their churches will bear their own individual stamp. These churches will then attract a following, and in some instances they will multiply their churches throughout a region.

There are real consequences for this kind of Christianity. Prior to the rise of contemporary individualistic churches, most churches were grounded in a theology of church government—Catholic, Episcopal, Presbyterian, Baptist etc.—but today's emerging churches derive their identity from individual leaders. Consequently, many Christians are gathering around the personality and vision of an individual. This has implications for the unity of the local church. Instead of local church unity being built upon the Scriptures, and biblical doctrines, contemporary church unity flows from individual conformity to the vision and ambition of the leader.

How does this affect the Scriptures and the doctrine of

Sola Scriptura? Quite simply it creates a situation where the truths of Scripture are filtered through the primary leader of the local church. Scripture means what the leader says it means. Consequently, the post-reformation church finds itself very close to the situation that the church was in prior to the reformation—the interpretation of the Scriptures is in the hands of the clergy. Only this time it's not popes and bishops who hold the keys to the kingdom, it is contemporary apostles and pioneers.

There is another way in which western individualism has left its mark on the church. The individualistic west is a consumer culture. People choose their church like they choose their coffee brands. Very often, doctrinal commitments are the last thing that people think about when they choose a church. Instead people are looking at other factors such as the style of the music, the children's work, and the social dynamics of the church. Given the fact that various denominations and new churches are all designing similar 'shop-windows' (contemporary band, motivational talk, full programmes) doctrines and government seem pretty much irrelevant. Consequently, these local Christians, who gather in local churches, are bound together not essentially by shared biblical convictions but by nothing other than their personal choice to commit to that particular church fellowship. This has a tremendous impact on the unity of a local church. Instead of Christians being united in their faith, church communities are a gathering place of individuals with diverse and often conflicting beliefs.

Again, what does this have to do with the doctrine of

Scripture? Everything. Many Christians are gathering in churches that claim the Bible is the highest authority. However, in reality, where there is no shared consensus amongst leaders and congregations regarding the interpretation of the Scriptures, it is not the Scriptures which have the highest authority, but individuals' opinions about Scripture. In this scenario, the preacher preaches his opinion, and individuals filter the message through their own personal worldview. In this sense, the modern evangelical church is very similar to Israel in days of old, 'In those days there was no king in Israel. Everyone did what was right in his own eyes.' (Judges 21:25).

The individualization of the church is one of the reasons why there is a lack of authority in the church. The preaching of the Word of God has been reduced to the opinion of man. Whether it be the dominant interpretation of an apostolic visionary, or the divided house of individualistic evangelicalism, the authority of Scripture suffers in these contexts. This is why the doctrine of *Sola Scriptura* is so important, it delivers the church from the shackles of human opinion and speculation, and it protects the church from the popish decrees of modern apostles. The Westminster Confession again demonstrates this:

> The supreme judge by which all controversies of religion are to be determined, and all decrees of councils, opinions of ancient writers, doctrines of men, and private spirits, are to be examined, and in whose sentence we are to rest, can be no other but the Holy Spirit speaking in the Scripture.[5]

Response

It was the recovery of Scripture which led to the reformation of the church, and it is the neglect of Scripture which is contributing to the deformation of the church. The only solution to the contemporary situation is for the church, and individuals to get back to the Book. On the day of judgement, it will not be the churches with the best brand or band that will be able to stand—it will be the churches which have been built on the right foundation. There is only one foundation for the church and that is the Word of God, all other foundations are sinking sand. Paul made this clear to Timothy when he revealed that true churches are built upon and defined by the truth of God's Word: If I delay, you may know how one ought to behave in the household of God, which is the church of the living God, a pillar and buttress of the truth. (1 Timothy 3:15).

Chapter Five: Radical Identity

'There's no God, now stop worrying and enjoy life'[1] claims the atheist. We 'aint nothing but mammals'[2] so let's get on with the business of sexual experimentation, sings the pop artist. I'm nothing more than a 'material girl'[3] living for material pleasures of a material world claims the singer. And as another young musician insightfully expressed—if matter is all there is, then nothing matters.[4]

The existence or non-existence of God changes everything. God is not just some abstract concept that has no relevance to the world in which we live; the existence of God has a direct effect on who we are and what we do. The Bible teaches this, and current societal trends prove it. Our identity and our behaviour are inseparably linked. They are not only linked, but they also defined by the existence or non-existence of God. If God does exist it changes everything. The existence of God directly affects who we are and how we should live. The rejection of God also has a direct consequence on how we understand our humanity

77

and how we live. The God question is inseparable from morality. What we believe about God will impact upon how we understand ourselves, others, the world and what we consider to be right and wrong.

Cultural Shift

The western world is in the process of a major morality shift. Laws are being radically revised. What was illegal yesterday is legal today. What was considered a social norm yesterday, is marginalized today. We are of course thinking in terms of gender, sexuality and marriage. What we are witnessing are the moral consequences of the cultural shift from morality which is based upon the Judaeo-Christian worldview (the Bible) to a morality that is derived from a secular humanistic worldview. In the previous chapter we looked at how humanism denies the supernatural and the after-life and constructs its own morality. What we are seeing in the present sexual, gender and marriage revolution is the outworking of humanistic morality. Our society previously derived its morality from the Scriptures. However, with the rejection of God, we now see the breakdown of human identity. If there is no God—our life has no ultimate meaning. We have no ultimate value. We have no worth. Even the love we have for those who are dearest to us is ultimately meaningless—it's nothing other than evolutionary, chemical and organic processes.

The Scriptures not only reveal God, but also reveal core truths about human identity, purpose and moral boundaries. We see that God does not just create life, but he also defines our identity, perimeters and purpose. We see this in the opening chapters of Genesis. However, Genesis does not just tell us our origins, it also explains our identity.

Identity

> So God created mankind in his own image,
> in the image of God he created them;
> male and female he created them. (Genesis 2:27)

There is no other worldview that gives men and women the dignity, worth and value that the Bible gives. The great irony is that people are rejecting Christianity for secular humanism because they think it gives them more equality. They believe that the concept of God and the commands of God rob them of their dignity and right to self-determination. Of course, the secularist humanists end up with a form of equality—but it's the equality of a brick in a wall—a rigid, lifeless and conforming equality. Consequently, they rob themselves of the knowledge of the beauty, freedom and uniqueness of a human being made in the image of the all-loving and all-powerful God.

> For you formed my inward parts; you knitted me together in my mother's womb. I praise you, for I am fearfully and wonderfully made. Wonderful are your works; my soul knows it very well. (Psalm 139:13,14)

Secular humanism claims to value human life, but with the removal of God, humanism loses any meaningful foundation for the value of human life. The Biblical view of humanity on the other hand safeguards the value, dignity and sanctity of life. It is no coincidence that it is our secular humanistic culture which gives humans the right to kill babies in the womb, and individuals the right to commit suicide. This is the logical outworking of a worldview that reduces humanity to matter.

Why does God hate gays and women?

Having worked with young people for approximately fifteen years, I often encounter the question, 'Why is God sexist?' or 'Why is God homophobic?' Such a question springs from a worldview that has been influenced and shaped by the media. God does not hate women, and God does is not homophobic. However, God is a great creator and designer, and as our creator and designer he is the One who has determined how life functions and works. The Biblical worldview is not a negative worldview, it is a positive worldview. The Bible reveals not only that we are individuals made in God's image with great value and worth, it also reveals how we should live in order that we may enjoy the blessing of God and fullness of life.

I remember exploring the opening passages of Genesis with a group of teenagers. We were reading about the creation of Eve.

But for Adam no suitable helper was found. [21] So the Lord God caused the man to fall into a deep sleep; and while he was sleeping, he took one of the man's ribs and then closed up the place with flesh. [22] Then the Lord God made a woman from the rib he had taken out of the man, and he brought her to the man.

[23] The man said,

'This is now bone of my bones
and flesh of my flesh;
she shall be called 'woman,'
for she was taken out of man.'

24 That is why a man leaves his father and mother and is
united to his wife, and they become one flesh.

'So that's why Christians don't agree with homosexuality!'
exclaimed one of the young people. We hadn't even
discussed anything, I hadn't taught anything—and the
aim of the session wasn't even about sexuality. She wasn't
a Christian, she didn't believe in God, but she was able to
understand from that small section of Genesis that God
created humans male and female for a specific purpose.
The purpose of male and female relationships is positive
and not negative, the reason that Christians cannot accept
alternative forms of sexuality is simply down to the fact
that all other forms of sexual relations depart from God's
purpose, pattern and perimeters.

It's no accident today that we are seeing *en masse*
confusion in terms of sexuality, gender and relationships.
There is an illusion that we are the ones who determine
the moral boundaries of our lives. However, it is God, and
not us who determines the boundaries. The biblical pattern
is that God has made men and women equal in value but
unique in their roles and identities. The biblical context
for sexual union is the covenant of marriage between one
man and one woman. If the world is going to be reached
for Christ—the biblical pattern needs to be rediscovered in
the church, in order that it can be modelled in the world.
Instead of being over-bearing and dominating, or passive

and disengaged—men are called to lovingly lead their families and be the head of their households. Men are to love their wives as Christ loved the church, and women are to submit to their husbands out of reverence for Christ.

> Now as the church submits to Christ, so also wives should submit in everything to their husbands. Husbands, love your wives, as Christ loved the church and gave himself up for her. (Ephesians 5:24–25)

Many Christians are wakening up to the fact that there is a major problem now that we are witnessing gay marriage in society and in the church. However, the reality is many churches abandoned God's purposes for marriage a long time before gay marriage appeared on the scene. The church began to lose the fight when it abandoned the unique and distinct roles of men and women. It lost the fight when it turned a blind eye to sex-before-marriage; it fled from the fight when adultery and divorce became widely accepted facts of life. It lost the fight when it turned away from the apostolic instructions about church leadership:

> I do not permit a woman to teach or to exercise authority over a man; rather, she is to remain quiet. (1 Timothy 2:12)

Again all of this is the result of *Scripture alone* being substituted by *culture alone*. If the Bible is not the inspired, authoritative, and sufficient Word of God, we are free to make up the rules as we go along. We are free to follow the trends of culture. However, if the Bible is the Word of God, we are not free to abandon Scripture—we are bound by it and have a responsibility to be faithful to it.

Purpose

Our purpose flows from our identity. Humans are created with worth and dignity, but in contrast to the humanist worldview which claims 'man is the measure of all things', we have been created with a greater purpose. The Westminster Shorter Catechism expresses our purpose this way:

> Q1: What is the chief end of man?
>
> A: Man's chief end is to glorify God, and to enjoy him for ever. (WSC)

The idea of enjoying God is completely foreign to most unbelievers. Their view of God is negative. They perceive Christianity to be all about rules, regulations and restrictions. The reality could not be further from the truth. We were created to know and enjoy God. Think about it, it would be strange if God created us as creatures with the ability to enjoy natural pleasures if our main purpose—knowing God—was something that was a drag and not a delight. The truth is, there is no greater delight, pleasure or joy to be found in this world that can be compared to the soul satisfying reality of knowing God.

Christians are not only called to enjoy God, we are called to glorify him, but what does this mean, and how are we to glorify God? The Westminster Shorter Catechism is again helpful in this area.

> Q. 2. What rule hath God given to direct us how we may glorify and enjoy him?
>
> A. The Word of God, which is contained in the Scriptures

of the Old and New Testaments, is the only rule to direct us how we may glorify and enjoy him.

Q. 3. What do the Scriptures principally teach?

A. The Scriptures principally teach, what man is to believe concerning God, and what duty God requires of man.[5]

The catechism is helping us understand that the key to connecting with our purpose is the Word of God. As we allow Scripture to shape our beliefs, and govern our choices, we will be aligned with our purpose—we will enjoy God and glorify him. However, as our culture shifts further towards secular humanism, the more biblically faithful Christians will be at odds with the current cultural values and behaviours. The pressure is on for everyone to embrace the new worldview, those who don't risk being labelled haters, bigots and discriminators.

LGBT Social Trends

Lesbian, Gay Bi-sexual and Transgender supporters have led a powerful campaign. In my lifetime, I've observed a cultural paradigm shift in terms of societal attitudes towards LGBT issues. For anyone who was actually gay, the 80s and 90s was a terrible time to grow up. If there was the slightest suspicion that a teenage boy was gay, he would be subject to a barrage of abuse.

In High School, I actually experienced something of the social hostility that surrounded people who were gay. When I was in 1st year, around the age of 12, a couple of senior pupils started a rumour claiming my best mate and I were gay. What began as a couple of senior pupils hurling insults grew into a year group and in turn spread through the entire high school. The jungle drums were effective; it wasn't long before 'news' spread to the other High School about a mile way. Within a matter of months, it is no exaggeration to say that the rumour spread throughout the entire community.

As a result, both of us individually encountered mocking, hostility and at times physical attacks. Both of us lived in different housing-schemes, but scattered throughout the various schemes were several gangs. Both of us struggled to go anywhere for a period of almost two years. If we were walking down the streets, I'd hear snickering, or people shouting 'poof' or 'faggot' and a host of other insults. Both of us individually encountered social hostility, isolation and violence.

At the time it was horrific, but looking back I realize that it has given me an insight into something of the abuse, and discrimination that some gay people may encounter at some point in their life. In this sense, as Christians, it is important to recognize that there are positive elements to the shift in cultural attitudes. Whilst Christians may not agree with homosexuality, the Bible does not endorse the hatred or ill-treatment of anyone because of their sexuality. The Bible calls us to even higher ground than toleration; it calls us to love our neighbour—no matter what the sexual-orientation of our neighbour is. From this perspective we should be glad that the LGBT campaign has reduced the hostile attitudes towards people who are part of the LGBT community.

One of the landmarks of the LGBT campaign has been

the redefinition of marriage. Marriage was redefined in England and Wales in 2013. The new Act allowed 'same-sex couples to marry in religious ceremonies, where the religious organization has "opted in" to conduct such ceremonies and the minister of religion agrees' and is designed to 'protect those religious organizations and their representatives who don't wish to conduct marriages of same-sex couples from successful legal challenge.'[6]

Whilst it is good that the government is not forcing churches to perform gay marriages, the new legislation has created a complicated cultural situation for churches and individual Christians. In order to give gay people the right to marriage, the government has had to redefine the meaning of marriage. Whilst Christians have to accept the fact that there is a new legal definition, their consciences forbid them to accept this definition of marriage. However, whilst 'religious organizations and their representatives' have a degree of protection, for the moment, individual members of churches do not. Consequently, in the public sphere, there is extreme social, legal, and political pressure to accept the new definition of marriage. To refuse to accept it or to speak out against it is to risk severe social and legal backlash.

The recent Ashers Baking Company row is a recent example of the current complexity surrounding this issue. In 2014 Ashers Baking Company, run by Christians, were asked to bake a cake with the words, 'Support Gay Marriage.' When the bakers refused to do so, it led to complaints being filed with Equality Commission and the couple who own the company being taken to court.

The court ruled that they had 'breached political and sexual orientation discrimination regulations' and fined the company £500. [7] The verdict was appealed, and the appeal was rejected. The whole case, and ruling is a clear indication of how the new attitudes towards LGBT issues are currently being outworked in the public sphere. The default position seems to be that Christians are being forced to accept gay marriage as valid, conscientious Christians are being silenced; all opposition to gay marriage and homosexual practice is censored and in some instances, as with the Ashers, Christians are being forced to actively approve of and promote gay marriage.

There are multitudes of current examples that demonstrate there is something of a censoring of Christian sexual ethics being brought out in public. In addition to the cake row, there have been café owners warned by police for displaying Bible verses[8], and street preachers have been arrested for preaching the Bible in public spaces.[9] In many of these cases, the charges are eventually dropped, but the very fact that complaints lead to immediate warnings or arrest clearly demonstrates that the odds are not stacked in the favour of Christians. Arrest first, find out the facts later seems to be the default position.

Chapter Six: Radical Relationships

How should the church respond to the present cultural challenges? There are no easy answers. Our individual responses will very much depend upon the particular challenges we are facing. However there are principles to be applied and pitfalls to be avoided. Biblical faithfulness is a narrow path with pitfalls on either side. We want to avoid the angry, hate-filled fundamentalism on the one hand, but on the other hand we want to avoid compromise and conformity to the status quo. If we choose to isolate ourselves whilst cursing the darkness, we fail in our missional mandate to be salt and light. If we accept the new humanistic morality we have compromised our Biblical convictions, thrown down our cross, trampled over it and embraced the path of apostasy.

There are three essential principles that each individual Christian, each local church, and every Christian family should embrace. As Christians we need to be determined to love people, resist the cultural agenda, and challenge the cultural agenda. We need to differentiate between people who are gay and pro-gay ideology. If we confuse the ideology with the person we risk losing the person. Likewise, we don't have to embrace the ideology in order to accept the person. Liberals and aggressive fundamentalists suffer from the same problem; they fail to embrace the tension.

Love the people

Our current culture is defining people by their sexual orientation; the LGBT community also define themselves by their sexuality. As Christians, we should look at the bigger picture. Instead of seeing people as gay and straight, and accepting the presumption that this is the all-defining issue, we need to see people as human beings made in the image of God. When the Pharisees looked at the woman who came and wept at Jesus feet, they saw a prostitute, but Jesus saw brokenness. When the Religious elite wanted to stone the adulterous women, all they saw was a sinner yet Jesus saw a woman in need of grace. We need to remember that sexual orientation is simply one aspect of a person's life; it is not the whole story. Jesus is interested in the whole person, not just one aspect of their life.

People's greatest need is reconciliation with God. This is true of gay people, straight people and transgender people. To be sure, sexual sin is serious, but it is not the only sin that a person has in his or her life. Rosaria Butterfield was an atheist-lesbian-professor who is now a Christian who is married to a Reformed pastor. She makes the point that Christians should not 'make moral proclamations in place of gospel invitations.'[1] In other words, if our LGBT neighbour thinks that Christianity is a moral code instead of an invitation to come to know God—we have failed to communicate the gospel. The gospel is not a moral code to be applied; it is good news to be received. And the good news is that although all people have sinned, all people can receive mercy through faith in Christ.

> All have sinned and fall short of the glory of God, and all are justified freely by his grace through the redemption that came by Christ Jesus. (Romans 3:23–24)

Most Christians today will have some contact with people who identify with the LGBT community. Part of the challenge for the Christian is to break down the cultural barriers and show friendship. LGBT people need to know that Christians don't hate them, Christians aren't afraid of them and that Christians love them. This does not mean we need to redefine our sexual ethics in order to comply with the new morality, it does mean we need to walk the tightrope of holding on to our convictions whilst loving the person. Rosaria Butterfield says,

> How can you possibly have strong words without strong relationships? And how can you possibly have strong relationships without taking the risk of being rejected? If you want to put the hand of the lost into the hand of the Saviour, you have to get close enough to get hurt. That may be a new idea for many Christians, but it's the ground rules of the new game.[2]

Butterfield is making the point that we can't communicate strong words if we don't have strong relationships. In other words, where there is opportunity, Christians should be open to building authentic relationships with their gay friends and neighbours. This will always carry the risk of being rejected. We live in a society that has been taught to think that rejection of a person's ideas is a rejection of the person. We need to try and show that this is not the case and that it is possible to love people without accepting or affirming sin.

The tensions are real. It becomes more of a reality when the issues emerge close to home. How do we respond when it's a family member who reveals that he or she is gay and is getting married to his or her partner? Should Christians attend gay weddings? Christians are already dividing over this issue. Those who argue in favour of attending gay weddings, make the point that Jesus went to weddings with sinners all the time. This is a similar argument that is put forward by Christians who think it was wrong for the Ashers to refuse to bake the cake that promoted gay marriage. To not bake the cake is considered to be discrimination, to not attend the wedding is to be viewed as a Pharisee.

However, it's one thing to be a 'friend of sinners' (we need to keep in mind we are all sinners) it's another thing to actively approve of something that goes against a commandment of God. Weddings, by their definition, are the celebration of a union. It is difficult to see how a Christian can attend a gay wedding without celebrating or approving something that God forbids.

Further, in attending a gay wedding celebration, Christians are accepting the idea that the ceremony is in fact a marriage, when it is not a marriage in the truest sense. The only marriage that the Bible recognizes is the union between a man and a woman. The state may declare that two men, or two women can be married, but that does not in any way make it a marriage before God. If Christians attend a same-sex ceremony they are embracing and promoting falsehood.

Finally, it would not be loving for a Christian to celebrate a gay wedding. In attending this celebration, the Christian is giving the impression that they are blessing and condoning the act. If Christians are Christ's ambassadors, this gives the impression that there is nothing serious about the lifestyle or the ceremony. The truth is there is something very serious taking place, there is a grievous sin being carried out against God. Jesus may have attended weddings with sinners, but Jesus never celebrated, approved or endorsed sin.

Of course, to claim to love a person yet at the same time to not attend their 'big day' is to risk severing the relationship. If there has been a genuine and loving relationship with the family member, and the wedding invitation is declined lovingly, and carefully we have done all that we can do to love the person and be faithful to the truth. The reality is, it's one thing to think about how to deal with this situation, it's another thing to be in the situation. This is especially so if it's a close family member, the closer the relationship, the deeper the pain, and the fiercer the tears.

Whilst the church is called to love the lost, it's important to stress that loving people involves truth-telling. It's tragic that liberal Christianity has hijacked the word 'love' and that 'love' has come to mean complete acceptance of both sin and sinner. However, this is not Biblical love. Biblical love is in perfect harmony with truth. Paul says, love 'does not rejoice at wrongdoing, but rejoices with the truth.' (1 Corinthians 13:6) What is the truth concerning homosexual behaviour? The truth is that it is a departure from God's pattern for human relationships, it is a rebellion against God's law and it brings serious judgement upon the person engaged in homosexual practice. Homosexual practice is listed as one of the sins that excludes a person from heaven, and brings a person under the eternal wrath of God.

> Or do you not know that the unrighteous will not inherit the kingdom of God? Do not be deceived: neither the sexually immoral, nor idolaters, nor adulterers, nor men who practice homosexuality. (1 Corinthians 6:9)

The big question that the media want an answer to from religious spokespersons, is what do they believe about homosexuality. The questions are direct, and pointed to allow as little political wrangling as possible. Of course, the media has an agenda, they want to label preachers as homophobic. The temptation in the midst of such social hostility is to avoid the issue altogether. But that will not do. Sooner or later we will have to deal with the issue. As Christians, we should take refuge in the Scriptures. The truth is, it is not us who say that homosexuality is a sin which invokes the wrath of God, it is God who says this. It is the Word of God which identifies homosexuality as sin, not us. Consequently, it is not us who are the judges, it is God.

However, we cannot stop here. Yes, homosexuality is a soul-destroying sin, but it's not an unforgivable sin. It is one of the many sins which brings God's wrath, but the person who is entangled in homosexual sin is not beyond God's grace. If we stop calling homosexuality sin, we remove the possibility for people trapped in this sin to find grace through repentance and faith. And this is part of the church's calling, to call all people, no matter what their sin, to repent of their sins and trust in Christ.

Resist the culture

As Christians we need to be firmly grounded in our identity and our purpose. Paul's exhortation to the Church in Rome is as applicable today as it ever was:

> Do not be conformed to this world, but be transformed by the renewal of your mind, that by testing you may discern what is the will of God, what is good and acceptable and perfect. (Romans 12:2)

Whilst the world is busy decorating their profile pictures with rainbows; and whilst hostile gay activists are looking for opportunities to censor Christians and force them to be conformed to the new morality, Christians need to stand strong. If our minds are transformed by the power of the Word of God, we will be given wisdom to know the will of God and strength to carry it out. If we simply go with the flow, we will be conformed to the world and we'll be resisting the purposes of God.

We need to remember that that this is not just a cultural or ideological battle; it is also a spiritual battle. Our enemies are not people; our enemies are spiritual enemies who oppose the Kingdom of God.

> 10 Finally, be strong in the Lord and in the strength of his might. 11 Put on the whole armour of God, that you may be able to stand against the schemes of the devil. 12 For we do not wrestle against flesh and blood, but against the rulers, against the authorities, against the cosmic powers over this present darkness, against the spiritual forces of evil in the heavenly places. 13 Therefore take up the whole armour of God, that you may be able to withstand in the evil day, and having done all, to stand firm. 14 Stand therefore, having fastened on the belt of truth, and having put on the breastplate of righteousness, 15 and, as shoes for your feet, having put on the readiness given by the gospel of peace. 16 In all circumstances take up the shield of faith, with which you can extinguish all the flaming darts of the evil one; 17 and take the helmet of salvation, and the sword of the Spirit, which is the word of God, 18 praying at all times in the Spirit, with all prayer and supplication. To that end keep alert with all perseverance, making supplication for all the saints. (Ephesians 6:10–18)

Resisting the cultural agenda

As Christians, we need to recognize the reality that people experience same-sex attraction and experience gender dysphoria. We need to engage in a loving and caring way towards people who identify themselves in such terms. However, we need to resist the current cultural philosophy that is seeking to deconstruct (and destroy) gender distinctions altogether. The current trend is leaning towards the rights of individuals to be able to choose their own gender, or non-gender, and the consequence of this is that established, traditional and Biblical understandings of gender roles are being destroyed.

This has an impact upon Education. Once gender-fluidity becomes government policy and the right of every individual, it then becomes the government's responsibility to ensure that every person, including children, are not having their rights violated. This kind of thinking can be seen in recent comments by the First Minister, Nicola Sturgeon who wants to introduce new legislation for adults, and children to choose their own gender.[3] The indoctrinating agenda can also be seen in the comments of Kezia Dugdale (MSP) who wants LGBT issues to be promoted not only in school Social Subjects, but *every* subject, including Maths and English.[4]

If the culture continues to go in its current direction, we will soon be in a situation where it will be a violation of sexuality and gender discrimination laws for Christians to raise their children in what used to be considered the natural way. To raise boys as boys, and girls as girls will be considered a violation of their human rights. *Who are we to force a gender on our children? We should wait until they are old enough to determine who or what they want to be.* This needs to be resisted, despite the cultural pressure to conform to an extremist social agenda. I'm not saying we should ignore the fact that some people suffer from gender dysphoria, I am saying that we need to resist the totalitarian regime that would have us replace reality with delusion.

How do we resist the cultural pressure? We need to resist it in the home, the church, and where possible in society. We have already lost a lot of ground on the societal front, but it's important that we don't just buckle and bow down to the pressure to conform. The battle for society begins in the home. For too long, Christian parents have handed over the education and spiritual development of their children to school and church. We need to know that we have the primary responsibility for educating our children in the ways of God.

We also need to resist the temptation to allow political correctness to dominate the pulpit. Some churches have an illusion of relevance; their pulpit is full of contemporary illustrations from the latest trivia that is taking place in popular culture. However, sermons laced with pop culture references that don't actually tackle the burning social and moral issues of the day simply disguise cowardice in the pulpit with a veneer of relevance.

If your church is not actively engaging biblically with the contemporary issues surrounding morality, identity and sexuality—you need to find a new church. If you are a preacher and you are shying away from these issues, you need to quit your job. Now is not the time for the faint-hearted, now is the time for the church to stand strong in the strength of the Lord.

Challenge the culture

The person and teaching of Jesus has always been controversial. The early church did not practice Christianity in the comfortable confines of Christendom. They lived out and spoke out their faith in a hostile culture. If we study Acts, we see that the early Christians endured hostility from Jewish and Gentile authorities. On one occasion the Jewish authorities attempted to censor the apostles. As the legislative authorities seek to censor Biblical teaching in the public spheres, we would do well to learn from the response of the apostles.

> They called them and charged them not to speak or teach at all in the name of Jesus. But Peter and John answered them, 'Whether it is right in the sight of God to listen to you rather than to God, you must judge, for we cannot but speak of what we have seen and heard.' (Acts 4:18–20)

How would we respond? This is no longer a hypothetical question. It's a current reality. Secular sexual ethics seeks to silence the Word of God. How are we responding? Are we conforming to the censorship? Are we playing the politically correct game where we speak in ambiguous language, in an attempt to feign faithfulness to the church, whilst conforming to the status quo? None of that will do. We are living in times that call for a humble, yet bold confrontation. As the world seeks to deconstruct our true identity and purpose, and construct a make-believe world of their own devising, we need to embrace the call of the prophet and call people back to their God-given identity and purpose.

See, I have set you this day over nations and over kingdoms, to pluck up and to break down, to destroy and to overthrow, to build and to plant. (Jeremiah 1:10)

Chapter Seven:
Radical Rebellion (Part One)

'Christianity? It's ridiculous—who is God to tell me what to do!' The answer was raw, bold and unashamedly honest. I was exploring faith and spirituality with a group of students and I had just asked the question, 'What immediately comes to mind when you think of Christianity?' I wasn't looking for eloquent and finely-honed answers—I wanted to capture gut instincts. Our initial reactions to a subject reveal a lot about our attitudes and values. This girl rejected Christianity, but her gut reason for doing so was incredibly insightful. I'm sure if I had given her a few weeks to prepare a talk, or an essay on her perspective on the Christian faith, I may have received a polished presentation that demonstrated the unscientific nature of faith, or the problem of evil, or the contradictions of Christianity, but the immediate gut-instinct response is in many ways more insightful—it gets to the heart of the matter. This girl was an atheist, not because there was a lack of evidence for God, she was an atheist because she didn't want God telling her how to run her life. Her problem with God was not a lack of evidence; her problem was authority.

Rebellion-driven atheism

In all the debates about the existence of God I've participated in, or observed over the years, I've noticed that there often comes a moment of honesty. It's a moment when the guard drops, and the arguments have run their course and the real issue comes to the surface. Put another way, it's when we see less of the arguments and more of the heart attitude—or we discover the belief that is really driving the person's atheism. In our example above, the reason for atheism was simply an unwillingness to accept God's authority, put bluntly; the atheism was driven by rebellion. We shouldn't be surprised at this, this is a core reason that the Bible gives for atheism. In other words, people don't reject God because there is a lack of evidence; people reject God because they refuse to submit to his authority.

The Gospel of John also demonstrates this principle, 'And this is the judgment: the light has come into the world, and people loved the darkness rather than the light because their works were evil.' (John 3:19) The Bible makes it clear that rejection of God is driven by an intentional suppression of the truth. We don't reject God because we cannot see the light; we reject God because we love the darkness.

The Bible shows us that the knowledge of God is

something that is made plain to each person, but each person fights against and resists this knowledge of God.

> ¹⁸ For the wrath of God is revealed from heaven against all ungodliness and unrighteousness of men, who by their unrighteousness suppress the truth. ¹⁹ For what can be known about God is plain to them, because God has shown it to them. ²⁰ For his invisible attributes, namely, his eternal power and divine nature, have been clearly perceived, ever since the creation of the world, in the things that have been made. So they are without excuse. ²¹ For although they knew God, they did not honour him as God or give thanks to him, but they became futile in their thinking, and their foolish hearts were darkened. (Romans 1: 18–21)

Paul is giving an overview of the pattern of rebellion against God. He is speaking in universal terms. Throughout the world people exchange the truth of God for a lie, they substitute true worship for false worship and light for darkness. The stark truth is this; we are living in a world which is shaking its fist towards heaven. We are living a world where the natural course is to resist the purpose of God.

We see this rebellion towards God everywhere. One recent example can be seen in Stephen Fry's raging attack against God. Fry claims that God is 'an utter maniac, totally selfish' and 'evil'. When questioned about what he would say to God if he were to die and discover that he did exist, he claims he would say, 'How dare you. How dare you create a world in which there is such misery that's not our fault? It's not right. It's utterly, utterly evil.' He then said, 'Why should I respect a capricious, mean-minded, stupid

God who creates a world which is so full of injustice and pain?'[1]

On a philosophical level, Fry is raising the 'Problem of Evil and Suffering'. His argument is not much different to that put forward by my hairdresser who once said, 'I just don't understand how God can exist alongside all the suffering in this world—why would he allow it?' Yet Fry's atheistic outburst reveals that there is more to his atheism than a philosophical problem. Fry hates God. Fry is raging against the character of God. He sees the suffering and injustice in the world, and he is projecting that onto God. He sees evil, and assumes that God is evil. If God is all-powerful, then surely he is to blame? However, whilst Fry is misunderstanding God's character, he *is* raging against God's authority. He is outraged that God allows evil and suffering. Fry's atheism, like all atheism, is a rebellion-driven atheism.

Another example of rebellion-driven atheism took place during a philosophy presentation. I had just presented the case that the science versus God argument was a myth. We had spent some time looking at arguments for the existence of God which were based upon the fine-tuning of the universe, and cosmology. We had reflected upon the statements of scientists who were theists. Having looked at a wide range of evidence, I asked the group, 'If science is not in conflict with the existence of God, and if science does not prove that God does not exist—why do many people embrace the popular notion that these sentiments are true?' One student's answer was priceless, 'Because I don't want God to exist'. There was a sense that she was realizing this truth for the first time. The girl was an atheist, she believed all the typical atheistic arguments, but in the context of looking at the evidence, discussing the issues, and reflecting on her own viewpoint, she came to the realization that she did not want God to exist. If God exists, we are accountable, and this is uncomfortable for those of us who are living our lives as if he did not exist. In this sense, the old saying is true, 'The atheist cannot find God for the same reason a thief cannot find a policeman.'

Original Rebellion

Secular humanists would have us think that humanity has reached a new dawn of enlightenment where we can discard the infantile restraints of religion. Humanity has come of age and is now more educated and equipped to deal with the reality of the world without the need for God. God may have been a helpful explanation for primitive cultures, but it has served its purpose and it is now no longer necessary. However, this is revisionist history of boldest kind. The history of humanity is a history of rebellion against God, not blind loyalty to God. Humanity has always gone astray, and there is nothing new about the new humanism other than the fact that it has hijacked scientific language to serve its own purposes. Human history is a story of human wandering and waywardness.

Atheistic philosophers put forth the 'Problem of Evil' as challenge to the existence of God. They boldly ask, 'If God is all-powerful, all-loving and all-knowing—why is there evil and suffering in the world? Surely if God is all-knowing he knows about all suffering and can prevent it; if he is all-loving surely he has the motivation to prevent it; and if he is all-powerful he has the ability to prevent it?' It sounds good, but the Problem of Evil and Suffering is not really a problem at all. It would be a problem if the Bible consisted of Genesis Chapter One—the End. But it doesn't—we have Genesis chapter Three—and that changes everything. When we look at the big picture of the whole Bible, we discover that human brokenness is at the heart of the Christian story—not in the margins. All evil and suffering find their source in Genesis chapter three, in the event known as The Fall. All historic and contemporary rebellion towards God has its source in the original rebellion which took place at the dawn of time. Understanding The Fall is essential if we are ever going to truly understand ourselves, our world and God.

We mentioned earlier that God created us with identity, purpose and moral parameters. For Adam, and his wife Eve, there was one simple law that God had given them. God had given them all they needed for life and happiness— he had entered a covenant with them—but the state of happiness was dependent upon Adam and Eve keeping the terms of the covenant. God had not created robots; he had made humans with the ability to choose. Adam and Eve, and all humanity would find their purpose in knowing God's love and loving God in return, but they would have to choose this—obedience to God was not forced upon them. God was interested in a relationship, and an obedience which flowed from a willingness to trust him. So God gave them one simple command, and their response to this command would determine the course of human history and experience.

The Lord God took the man and put him in the Garden of Eden to work it and take care of it. [16] And the Lord God commanded the man, 'You are free to eat from any tree in the garden; [17] but you must not eat from the tree of the knowledge of good and evil, for when you eat from it you will certainly die.' (Genesis 2:15)

The world that Adam and Eve initially inhabited was not the world that you and I know today. Their experience was initially free from pain, death and evil. Whilst God had given them a choice; he warned them of the consequences. We can see from the warning that there would be two effects if they rebelled—evil and death. In other words, evil and suffering would enter the world. The very things that Stephen Fry raged and ranted about—suffering and evil—were the very things that God warned Adam and Eve about. If we want to find a source of the world's injustice and pain, we don't find it in God, we find it in humanity. We find it in the rebellion of Adam. Along with paradise, God gave Adam and Eve a law and Adam and Eve responded just like our girl at the start of this chapter, 'Who is God to tell me what to do!'

The Fall

In Genesis Chapter Three we see the events which lead to up to the Fall.

Now the serpent was more crafty than any other beast of the field that the Lord God had made.

He said to the woman, 'Did God actually say, "You shall not eat of any tree in the garden"?' [2] And the woman said to the serpent, 'We may eat of the fruit of the trees in the garden, 3 but God said, "You shall not eat of the fruit of the tree that is in the midst of the garden, neither shall you touch it, lest you die."' 4 But the serpent said to the woman, 'You will not surely die. 5 For God knows that when you eat of it your eyes will be opened, and you will be like God, knowing good and evil.' 6 So when the woman saw that the tree was good for food, and that it was a delight to the eyes, and that the tree was to be desired to make one wise, she took of its fruit and ate, and she also gave some to her husband who was with her, and he ate. (Genesis 3: 1–6)

In order to understand what is going on here, it is helpful to skip forward to the end of the Bible. The book of Revelation, the last book in the Bible sheds some light on this event in Genesis—this first book of the Bible.

Now war arose in heaven, Michael and his angels fighting against the dragon. And the dragon and his angels fought back, 8 but he was defeated, and there was no longer any place for them in heaven. 9 And the great dragon was thrown down, that ancient serpent, who is called the devil and Satan, the deceiver of the whole world—he was thrown down to the earth, and his angels were thrown down with him. (Revelation 12:7–9)

It's difficult to say with any certainty when exactly the War in Heaven took place, but we are able to draw some conclusions. The rebellion on earth originated with a rebellion in heaven. When Satan, and his angels, rebelled against the Lord, they lost their place in heaven and took the war to the earth. The devil could not attack Adam and Eve, the only way the devil could wreak havoc on the earth was by leading Adam and Eve into the rebellion. In order to do this, he needed to deceive them.

Satan's tactic was an attack on the character of God. He led Adam and Eve to believe that God was lying to them—that God could not be trusted. He caused them to desire more than they already had—eating the fruit would not bring death, he promised, it would bring greater wisdom and status—they would be like God, they would determine what is right and wrong, they wouldn't need God to tell them the rules. They themselves could know and decide right from wrong. They bought the lie, and joined the dark side.

They didn't drop dead immediately. Was this proof that God had given them wrong information? No. The process of death began immediately. Adam and Eve immediately underwent a change in their experience. They become aware of their nakedness—they feel shame. They sense God drawing near, they run and hide. When God confronts them, they blame each other, so harmony is replaced with conflict. God pronounces judgements, the devil is condemned, Adam is told he will encounter hardship and frustration all the days of his life, Eve is told she will encounter pain as a mother, and conflict with her husband. Then, they are banished from the Garden of Eden—the tree of life is taken from them, they have lost everlasting life. Their own journey is now a slow journey towards death. Everything has changed. The environment becomes harsh, relationships are troubled and heartache and tragedy are part of human existence. In the future, Adam and Eve's two sons will experience this conflict, and one brother will murder the other. Evil and Suffering will now mark life for all future generations.

The Fall did not just affect life for Adam and Eve, the Fall affected life for every living creature, and every person ever to be born. Human identity was changed, instead of being righteous, by nature we are now sinners. Instead of living in harmony with God, we are now hostile to God. Instead of seeing God clearly, we are now blind to God. Instead of being spiritually alive, we are now spiritually dead. Instead of knowing eternal life in God's favour, we are destined for eternal punishment—hell. All of us by nature are radically rebellious towards God, and all of us are under the judgement of God, 'Therefore, just as sin came into the world through one man, and death through sin, and so death spread to all men because all sinned' (Romans 5:12)

We shouldn't be surprised by this. We know, even from a biological perspective, that a child's identity is influenced by the parents. We are a product of our parents. We share their genes. Characteristics of the parents are passed on to the children. Likewise, all of us are born with the characteristics of our first parents—all of us are born in sin, and into a world which is under the curse of the Fall.

The apostle Paul outlines the pattern of rebellion within human societies, and highlights the effect of the fall upon the whole creation. Regarding the creation he says,

> For the creation was subjected to futility, not willingly, but because of him who subjected it, in hope [21] that the creation itself will be set free from its bondage to corruption and obtain the freedom of the glory of the children of God. [22] For

we know that the whole creation has been groaning together in the pains of childbirth until now. (Romans 8:20–22)

In other words, the whole creation is suffering as a result of the fall. We know this to be true; we know how fragile the world is at times. News reports are constantly bringing to our attention the environmental dangers of our planet. The world and its people are broken.

Regarding the rebellious side to our nature, Paul outlines the downward spiral that occurs in human societies when the revelation of God is rejected. After establishing the fact that God's existence and character are self-evident through the creation, and all people know this despite the fact they suppress this truth, Paul goes on to show the consequences of writing God out of the story of our lives.

For although they knew God, they did not honour him as God or give thanks to him, but they became futile in their thinking, and their foolish hearts were darkened. 22 Claiming to be wise, they became fools, 23 and exchanged the glory of the immortal God for images resembling mortal man and birds and animals and creeping things.

24 Therefore God gave them up in the lusts of their hearts to impurity, to the dishonouring of their bodies among themselves, 25 because they exchanged the truth about God for a lie and worshipped and served the creature rather than the Creator, who is blessed for ever! Amen.

26 For this reason God gave them up to dishonourable passions. For their women exchanged natural relations for those that are contrary to nature; 27 and the men likewise gave up natural relations with women and were consumed

with passion for one another, men committing shameless acts with men and receiving in themselves the due penalty for their error.

28 And since they did not see fit to acknowledge God, God gave them up to a debased mind to do what ought not to be done. 29 They were filled with all manner of unrighteousness, evil, covetousness, malice. They are full of envy, murder, strife, deceit, maliciousness. They are gossips, 30 slanderers, haters of God, insolent, haughty, boastful, inventors of evil, disobedient to parents, 31 foolish, faithless, heartless, ruthless. 32 Though they know God's decree that those who practise such things deserve to die, they not only do them but give approval to those who practise them. (Romans 1: 22–32)

The downward spiral is this—we were made to worship, and when we reject God as the centre-point in our lives, we will worship something else. We will worship stuff, we will worship life, we will worship the things of the world, rather than the maker of the world. As we turn from God, we exchange the truth for a lie, and instead of giving glory to God, we give glory to ourselves or created things. Loss of identity, purpose and perimeters go hand in hand. A realigning of the sexual boundaries which God has put in place is the natural outworking of the rejection of God. Our fundamental sin is not so much what we do, but what we refuse to believe. By rejecting God, we are assaulting his character, and all our actions flow from this base. In other words, a godless worldview leads to a godless morality.

Chapter Eight:
Radical Rebellion (Part Two)

Humanism is the natural philosophy of fallen humanity. It is the devil's doctrine. Satan came to Adam and Eve with an empty promise, 'But the serpent said to the woman, "You will not surely die. For God knows that when you eat of it your eyes will be opened, and you will be like God, knowing good and evil."' (Genesis 3:4–5) The serpent was the first humanist philosopher, and Adam and Eve were the first converts. In Genesis chapter three we see the three basic elements of humanism that we mentioned previously.

First we see the denial of the divine, God is not a trustworthy source, take the fruit and recognize your human potential—*you* will be like God.

Humanists do not believe in a God or gods, or any other supernatural or divine entities. Humanists do not think that the universe needs a divine power outside of itself in order to have value. We, inside the universe, determine its value.

We think that other people, for example, are moral concerns, not because they are made in the image of Something Else, but because of who they are in themselves.[2]

Then, just like the humanist, the serpent is claiming that we don't need religious laws to tell us how to live our life; we can determine our own course of morality.

Humanism is an approach to life based on humanity and reason—humanists recognize that moral values are properly founded on human nature and experience alone and that the aims of morality should be human welfare, happiness and fulfilment. Our decisions are based on the available evidence and our assessment of the outcomes of our actions, not on any dogma or sacred text.[3]

The serpent also claims there is nothing to fear about death—'you will not die' said the serpent, just like the humanist who assures us, 'don't worry about that death stuff—there is no day of judgement, there is no afterlife.' This is the exact same claims made by humanists, 'Humanists believe that we have only one life, it is our responsibility to make it a good life, and to live it flourishingly.'[4] Humanism is not a new ideology, it's the age old rhetoric of rebellious humanity.

Humanism: the deification of humanity?

Humanism is a self-confessedly positive worldview. Humanism has a high view of humanity. The humanist manifesto could be summed up with the slogan, 'Man is the measure of all things.' Humanity, not deity is the centre-point of civilization. Humanism is positive about human potential:

- Humanists believe that people can and will continue to find solutions to the world's problems, so that quality of life can be improved for everyone.

- Humanists are positive, gaining inspiration from our lives, art and culture, and a rich natural world.[5]

This is where the lines begin to get blurred. As Christians, we can look at those two beliefs and find no fault. The Bible also depicts humanity as having great potential. However, the greatness of humanity was designed to be outworked in a particular context. Humans were made in the image of God, and they were created to reflect God's glory and greatness. However, when the devil told Adam and Eve that we could 'be like God' we reached beyond our station. We snatched a power that that is greater than our identity and purpose. We committed treason; we robbed for ourselves that which belongs to God alone. Consequently we have a higher view of ourselves than is actually true. We are pretenders to the throne. When Humanism claims 'Man is the measure of all things' it is taking for itself that which belongs to God alone: 'I am the LORD; that is my name; my glory I give to no other, nor my praise to carved idols.' (Isaiah 42:8)

Humanism fails to take into account human weakness, limitation and sinfulness. There is a destructive element to our creativity and potential. The same science which can be used to save lives is being used to destroy lives. The same human creativity which gives us the arts and music also gives us weapons and war. We devise ways to heal the sick through medicine, but we also design ways to destroy the lives of the unborn. Humanity is not Superman as humanism would have us believe, humanity is more like Dr Jekyll and Mr Hyde.

Humanism in the Church

The Bible's teaching on the human condition is incredibly unpopular in our society today. Humanism boasts in the greatness of human nature. Humanism celebrates human goodness, human potential and human goodness. To a self-assured humanistic culture, the idea that humans are sinful by nature, sinful in heart, and sinful in deed is a radical and prophetic rebuke. Society does not want to hear about sin, and neither do many quarters of the church. Even within evangelicalism there is a tendency to neglect or reject this teaching. Evangelicalism, in many parts of the West, has ceased calling sinners to repentance, and is instead celebrating the greatness of human potential. However, in order to see true gospel transformation, we need to understand the depth of the human problem: we are not just broken people in need of wholeness; we are rebels in need of redemption.

There are a number of ways that humanism is directly affecting the church. However, for the purposes of this chapter we will consider a few of the most significant areas.

Human-centred Bible teaching

The Bible is all about Jesus. Good Bible teaching is Christ-centred Bible teaching. The Scriptures, from Genesis to

Revelation, are designed to reveal God's unfolding plan of salvation. Consequently, good Bible teaching should point to Jesus. Jesus himself revealed this truth, 'You search the Scriptures because you think that in them you have eternal life; and it is they that bear witness about me' (John 5:39) and the greatest Bible teachers in the history of the church have understood the importance of Christ-centred preaching. Charles Spurgeon said,

> The motto of all true servants of God must be, 'We preach Christ; and him crucified.' A sermon without Christ in it is like a loaf of bread without any flour in it. No Christ in your sermon, sir? Then go home, and never preach again until you have something worth preaching.[6]

Contemporary evangelicalism lacks Christ-centred Bible teaching and preaching. This can be seen everywhere. Mega-church pastors move their audiences with compelling oratory excellence yet the central character in their sermons is often self, not Christ. Likewise, Biblical passages are often applied in a way that gives the hearers the impression that they, and not God, are the main players in salvation.

This is a trend that can be observed from the televised mega-church, to the small local church. We observe humanistic messages in the pulpit and the bookstores. A passing glance at some of the most popular Christian books is clear evidence that Christians are caught up in man-centred religion. Popular books are clear evidence that Christians are replacing God-help for self-help. Some of these titles are: *Approval Addiction: Overcoming Your Need to Please Everyone; Authentic Hope for the Disillusioned;*

The Me I Want to Be: Becoming God's Best Version of You;
Become a Better You: 7 Keys to Improving Your Life Every Day
and *When Will My Life Not Suck?*

Human-centred mission

The major impact of humanism upon the church can be
seen in how we view mission. The popular saying, usually
wrongly attributed to Saint Francis of Assisi, has become
the benchmark of orthodoxy in many churches, 'Preach the
gospel always, and if necessary use words.' This philosophy
is often used to justify a means to mission which is centred
on social action, rather than gospel proclamation. In many
churches throughout the UK, Street Teams go out in
droves in order to meet the needs of revellers, homeless
and prostitutes. Likewise Christian based charities carry
out support work with young people, families, children and
addicts. These services often do a great work, and it is the
Christian thing to do, but they also often receive funding
from secular sources. The outcome of this is that many of
these ministries become shaped by the ethos, values and
principles of a secular body. Consequently, the church's
acts of mercy and compassion become divorced from the
missional impetus to reach the lost and make disciples.

The gospel message has also taken a beating in recent
years. We will look at this more closely in the next chapter,
but for now it is enough to say that the subject of sin has
largely been removed from the message of the gospel.
As the above book titles indicated, the gospel is often
presented as a means of self-improvement rather than the
means by which we are saved from sin and God's wrath and

saved for the Glory of God. In a way that is fully compatible with the values of humanism, the gospel is presented as a recipe for people to reach their full potential.

The reality that many people are interpreting the gospel as a way to improve personal potential, hit home powerfully one night at a church service. I was scheduled to speak at a church in another city. I decided to take a young person from the youth group along with me, and I asked her to share her testimony. I had heard that she had a 'good testimony', and that she had gone from being a young person full of self-hatred, to a young person full of joy with a passion for God.

When the girl stood up and gave her testimony, it was encouraging to hear how her life had been turned around, but there were a few things which really struck me. The essence of her message was about how she now had hope because she understood that God loved her and had a plan for her life, and that she was 'soooo looking forward' to God helping her to become a 'Rock Star.' And that was it. The end. What was missing? Just about every essential element of the Biblical gospel. There was no reference to her ever having been convicted of sin, understanding the good news that Jesus died for sins, and how she came to trust Christ and experience an assurance of salvation. All of that was absent. This is isn't the only time I've noticed this, almost every time I listen to a Christian testimony, I notice the same problem. Whilst it is great that some ministries are engaging with people and helping them change their lives, the reality is the gospel is not being communicated faithfully or effectively. This is itself is one of the reasons why many people fall away after a short period of time. They have bought into a false gospel. The gospel of human potential is not the gospel of the New Testament.

The root of humanity's problem is a default heart condition which is in rebellion towards God. The Gospel is designed to deal with the root problem. Any gospel message which does not get to the root of our rebellion is inadequate. The modern gospel invites people to accept Jesus whilst continuing to cling to their idols. The rebel's cry is 'who is God to tell me what to do!' Any gospel message which doesn't strike at the heart of this idol is a humanistic counterfeit that empowers us to maintain the illusion that we are the lords of our own lives.

Chapter Nine:
Radical Rescue (Part One)

There are many challenges facing the 21st century church, and the cross of Christ is one of the greatest battlegrounds. Genesis to Revelation is the great unfolding of God's plan of rescue, redemption and reconciliation. It's the story of a father seeking lost sons, a husband pursuing a wayward bride and shepherd bringing home his wandering sheep. At the Fall, humanity becomes a rebel under God's wrath; at the cross, the Son of God becomes the Rebel's righteousness. In Genesis Chapter Three, God warned Adam that his sin would result in death; at the cross Jesus dies the rebel's death in order to rescue rebels from the wrath of God. This is the Good News of the Gospel. However, not everyone sees the cross as good news. The cross is offensive to both the religious and the rationalist. The words of the Apostle Paul are as true today as they were two thousand years ago, 'For many, of whom I have often told you and now tell you even with tears, walk as enemies of the cross of Christ.' (Philippians 3:18)

The teaching of the cross (in theological terms, the atonement) is in crisis in several specific ways. In some cases the theology of the cross is under attack from critics inside and outside the church; in other places the message of the cross is simply omitted from gospel preaching and church teaching; and in other contexts the teaching of the cross is twisted. Humanists, liberal ministers, and pseudo-evangelicals have launched their attacks on the cross calling it a form of 'cosmic child abuse';[1] mainstream evangelicals by-pass the cross, preferring instead to talk about a 'life transforming relationship with Jesus'; churches influenced by Word of Faith teaching have redefined the cross as a slot machine which churns out health, wealth and success, and other evangelicals are happy to speak of the cross as testimony to our worth, but not as a testimony to our wickedness. These four trends have redefined the way that Christians think about the cross. Consequently, very few churches preach the cross of Christ in a biblical way. On the whole, the old theology of the cross is seen as abusive, and as a result preaching of the cross is altogether absent, or is redefined in such a way that the cross becomes a means of affluence or affirmation. Very few are willing to preach the cross as the means of atonement.

The Abusive Cross

A prominent Church of Scotland Minister was asked the question, 'Do you believe that Jesus died for your sins?' His response? 'No! No! No! No! That's ghastly theology; you don't want to go there!' The Minister recalled this incident in a sermon, the sermon was uploaded on to YouTube, and the blogosphere was set ablaze. A Church of Scotland Minister was publically denying the historical, universal and biblical teaching of the cross. The Minister did not stop at denying the doctrine, he went on to declare full-scale war on the doctrine of the atonement, referring to it as 'past its sell-by-date' and 'immoral'.

> Jesus' death is foundational for Christianity and there is a widespread understanding that He died in our place: Jesus paid the price for our sins. In my view, this theology is an obstacle to evangelism in the 21st century. It is an obstacle because it portrays God as a potentate who demands blood for offences He has suffered: our sins have offended him and he demands a blood sacrifice ... Known as substitutionary atonement, because Jesus is our substitute, he dies the death we deserve, God's forgiveness is 'applied' to us. In this theology, Christ is an atoning sacrifice and, on account of Jesus' death, a propitiation or ransom for sin, God chooses to see us as righteous. His wrath is satisfied. I'm almost embarrassed explaining this theology because it is well past its 'sell by date' and, in some sense, is immoral ... Jesus never asked His followers to believe in a creed or His divinity. Instead, he called them to 'faith' ... We must discard outdated theology.[2]

According to this Minister, and other progressives, the message of the cross, as preached by the apostles, is a hindrance to mission, a misrepresentation of the character of God, and immoral to the core. In other words, it's not helping evangelism because people don't want to hear a message of retribution, justice and sin; it's portraying God as barbaric, and it goes against all that people consider to be good and true. However, the question we need to ask ourselves is this, is the message of the cross Biblical? Is the doctrine of substitutionary atonement Biblical? If it is Biblical, and I would argue that it is, then it is actually the progressive and liberal representation of the cross that is a hindrance to evangelism, an attack on the character of God and immoral. The liberal cross hinders evangelism because it removes the only means by which people can be saved— the message of the cross, it attacks God's character because it does not present a God who is Holy and Just, and it is immoral because it calls that which God calls good evil.

Liberals are 'embarrassed' by the message of the cross, and they consequently seek to redefine it but we need to remember that the cross has always been a source of shame and scandal. At the time of Christ, and the early church, the cross was despised by Greeks and Jews alike.

> Where is the one who is wise? Where is the scribe? Where is the debater of this age? Has not God made foolish the wisdom of the world? For since, in the wisdom of God, the world did not know God through wisdom, it pleased God through the folly of what we preach to save those who believe. For Jews demand signs and Greeks seek wisdom, but we preach Christ crucified, a stumbling block to Jews and folly to Gentiles, but to those who are called, both Jews and Greeks, Christ the power of God and the wisdom of God. For the foolishness of God is wiser than men, and the weakness of God is stronger than men. (1 Corinthians 1:20–25)

The rationalist, and the religious, have always been

offended by the cross. The Greeks were the rationalistic humanists at the time of the early church, the Jews were the religious elites who were preoccupied with the praise of the people and popularity. Today, it is the atheistic humanist, and the religious progressives who oppose the cross. Humanists and progressives are not only found in the atheist camp, or the high church cathedrals, they are scattered throughout the 'evangelical' world. Consequently, for any preacher, church or Christian who desires to stand by the truth of the cross, the cost of doing so is high. To hold firm to the Biblical gospel is to risk ridicule, rejection and rage from the world and the worldly church. However, this has always been the mark of apostolic preaching. As modern 'apostles' are rebranding themselves and the church in a way that appeals to the cultural zeitgeist we must remember that apostolic Christianity has never appealed to the flesh of fallen humanity. Apostolic Christianity has always invoked the scorn and contempt of the wider culture.

For I think that God has exhibited us apostles as last of all, like men sentenced to death, because we have become a spectacle to the world, to angels, and to men. We are fools for Christ's sake, but you are wise in Christ. We are weak, but you are strong. You are held in honor, but we in disrepute. To the present hour we hunger and thirst, we are poorly dressed and buffeted and homeless, and we labor, working with our own hands. When reviled, we bless; when persecuted, we endure; when slandered, we entreat. We have become, and are still, like the scum of the world, the refuse of all things. (1 Corinthians 4:9–13)

An unbiased reading of the Bible will make it clear that the theology of the cross is central to the Bible's main message. What the progressives call 'ghastly theology' the Bible sets forth as 'the power of God and the wisdom of God'. Before we show from the Scriptures the clear evidence that Christ died for sinners as a substitutionary and atoning sacrifice, let us look at other theological trends that are undermining the true message of the cross.

The Absent Cross

Since my conversion in 1999, I've had experience with and exposure to many diverse ministries which reach out to young people and also people who are struggling with substance addiction. Throughout this period I have noticed a growing trend. Many ministry manifestos omit any mention of salvation; many gospel presentations by-pass the cross and multitudes of testimonies miss out the essentials of the gospel. I've heard hundreds of testimonies from people who have been delivered from alcohol and substance addiction. Many of these people have developed their own ministries and their testimonies are graphic accounts of how God has taken them from a place of hopelessness to a life of success. Today, testimonies are rarely about making Jesus famous, instead testimonies seem to be nothing more than 'rags to riches' stories with God thrown in as the support act. In modern testimonies it is often the case that the person giving testimony is the hero of their own story, God is simply a destiny-like character, in the background, working things out for the person's good.

What we are observing in modern evangelism is the influence of humanism upon the gospel message. If the gospel is purely all about personal transformation, the cross becomes less important—it becomes peripheral. The message of 'evangelism' becomes less about seeing people redeemed, rescued and reconciled; it simply becomes a message of personal and social transformation. Consequently the good news is no longer about eternity, it's all about improving your life here and now. The gospel is presented as a means to better self-esteem, better opportunities and higher quality of living.

The new evangelism resonates with the culture. To people in hopelessness, it offers not only hope—but the hope they are looking for. Biblical evangelism, on the other hand, is more of a challenge because it tells people what they need to hear, not only what they want to hear. The irony is, it is only the true gospel that will give people what they are truly longing for. The true preaching of the cross reconciles people to God, and when people are reconciled to God, they are receiving a new identity and a new purpose. They find everything they are looking for but it is only found in the one area they do not want to look— the cross of Christ.

When we substitute the true preaching of the cross, for a vague message of transformation, we deprive people of the very transformation they need. We substitute authentic, spiritual and eternal transformation for superficial and temporal transformation. On the other hand, when we present the true message of the cross, we offer a spiritual and eternal message, but it very often includes social and personal transformation too. When people get saved, they *do* feel better about themselves, they *do* have hope for the here and now, but only because the gospel is not about the here and now it's about eternity; they feel better about themselves, only because the gospel is not about them, it's about Jesus.

Does it actually matter, providing people are being reached for Christ? What does it matter if the cross is not being presented accurately, providing people are coming to Jesus and being 'set free'? It matters greatly. If the cross is not being preached, people are not being saved. They may be buying into religion, they may be dabbling in spirituality, they may even get themselves off drugs, but if the cross is not being preached, and people are not being called to repentance and faith, people are not being saved, they are being deceived. They are embracing a false gospel. Christianity without the cross is false Christianity, and a gospel without the cross is a false gospel. John Stott says it well when he says, 'There is then, it is safe to say, no Christianity without the cross. If the cross is not central to our religion, ours is not the religion of Jesus.' If we are giving people hope in the name of Jesus, without the cross, we are giving people false hope. And this is surely one of the greatest acts of cruelty. The Bible reserves the severest words for those who would redefine the message of the cross:

> I am astonished that you are so quickly deserting him who called you in the grace of Christ and are turning to a different gospel— not that there is another one, but there are some who trouble you and want to distort the gospel of

Christ. But even if we or an angel from heaven should preach to you a gospel contrary to the one we preached to you, let him be accursed. As we have said before, so now I say again: If anyone is preaching to you a gospel contrary to the one you received, let him be accursed. (Galatians 1:6–9).

Another reason that a correct emphasis on the cross matters has to do with discipleship. I have no doubt that many people who profess faith in Christ through drug crisis ministries genuinely come to Christ. God works through broken vessels. And he can use inadequate presentations of the gospel for his own glory. However, the consequences for discipleship are tragic. Many people profess faith in Christ, but they are given very weak foundations. Consequently their Christian life is marked by immaturity. An influx of new Christians brought into the church with weak methods leads to weak and confused churches. The Bible warns against this:

For no one can lay a foundation other than that which is laid, which is Jesus Christ. Now if anyone builds on the foundation with gold, silver, precious stones, wood, hay, straw—each one's work will become manifest, for the Day will disclose it, because it will be revealed by fire, and the fire will test what sort of work each one has done. If the work that anyone has built on the foundation survives, he will receive a reward. If anyone's work is burned up, he will suffer loss, though he himself will be saved, but only as through fire. (1 Corinthians 3:11–15)

When examined in the light of Scripture, it seems clear that many modern ministries are building their churches on faulty foundations and superficial materials. The Word of God is clear, we should be concerned with what we are building, and how we are building. However, because we have ceased to measure success with Biblical criteria, but instead are measuring success with worldly criteria, we have reached a stage where the church does not even know there is a problem. If the numbers measure up, everyone is happy. If thousands of people are coming to Christ, God must be happy with us, right? Not essentially. The above Scripture should remind us that God is not only interested in quantity, but quality. If our ministry is not centred in Christ, and preparing people for eternity—our ministry will bear no fruit in the end. We are living in times when there is great reward in being seen to be a humanitarian. For those of us who are involved in helping people, we need to be careful that we have not received our reward here and now at the expense of the eternal reward.

Chapter Ten:
Radical Rescue (Part Two)

The cross is not peripheral in all expressions of evangelicalism, in some ministries the centrality of the cross is maintained but it is misrepresented. The cross, it is claimed, is the means by which believers can enter into a life free from sin, sickness, debt and defeat. The cross is a vehicle that leads us to victorious Christian living. We are of course speaking about the prosperity gospel. As I write this chapter, prosperity Preacher, Creflo Dollar is scheduled to speak in Scotland. He has been invited by a contemporary charismatic church which is based in Scotland but is expanding its influence through national and international church planting. In a recent social media update, Dollar claimed: 'Jesus bled and died for us so that we can lay claim to the promise of financial prosperity.'[1]

Due to the influence of Christian TV stations, bookstores, and the internet, prosperity teaching has subtly worked its way into almost every section of the church.

Joyce Meyer, T.D. Jakes, Hillsongs, Joel Osteen and Joseph Prince are popular ministries enjoyed by Christians of every denominational stripe, and they all have one thing in common—prosperity theology. Because their ministries use Biblical language to promote faulty teaching, many Christians are unaware that these ministries are in fact false teachers. They have corrupted the Biblical message of the cross by presenting it as a means to health, wealth and success.

The Affirming Cross

The church tends to be a bit like a pendulum, it swings in extremes. For the last six years I've been living in the Scottish Highlands. The Highlands are Presbyterian land. Sadly, as well as leaving a legacy of revivals, some expressions of Scottish Presbyterianism have left a legacy of legalism. Historically, people have understood the message of the church to be, 'The good news is you are going to hell'. Highland Christianity had a tendency to be more sin-focused than Christ-focused. Contemporary evangelicalism has reacted to this kind of negative Christianity, but the pendulum has swung full-speed in the opposite direction. I recently heard a preacher on Christian television say, 'The cross, isn't the revelation of my sin, the cross is the revealing of my value'.[2] This is a shocking perversion of the cross, but it is a common misrepresentation. For many evangelicals, sin is a symptom of poor self-esteem, and the cross is the means to a greater self-esteem. The truth is, as mentioned in a previous chapter, our value comes from being made in the image of God, but we have become deeply corrupted. So much so, that the price for our sin was the cross of Christ. The cross is a revelation of our sin. If our sin can only be paid by the suffering and death of Christ, how evil must we be? Consequently, the cross is a revelation of God's mercy, grace and love, and a revelation of our sin. We are not supposed to look at the cross and feel better about ourselves, we are supposed to look at the cross and be convicted of our sin.

The new cross

Due to the unpopularity of the cross, evangelicals are either by-passing the cross, or redefining it. The redefinition of the cross is not a new problem within evangelicalism; A.W. Tozer perceived the corruption of the message of the cross is his day:

> The old cross slew men; the new cross entertains them. The old cross condemned; the new cross amuses. The old cross destroyed confidence in the flesh; the new cross encourages it. The old cross brought tears and blood; the new cross brings laughter.[3]

Tozer's observations about the new cross are as relevant today as they were in his own day. One of the greatest needs of the hour is a rediscovery of the Biblical preaching of the cross. Central to understanding the cross is our understanding of the seriousness of sin and the holiness of God. John Stott helps us understand the importance of this, 'Before we can begin to see the cross as something done for us we have to see it as something done by us.'[4]

God's Radical Rescue Plan

Understanding the cross correctly is essential because the cross is God's solution to a broken world. In the previous chapter, we saw that sin led to judgement and condemnation for the human race. However, the fall did not take God by surprise, God knew Adam would sin even before the world was created, and he designed a rescue plan—a rescue plan that was formed in the heart and mind of the Trinity before the world began.

The Bible, from beginning to end, reveals the radical rescue plan of God. In the first book of the Bible, right after Adam and Eve sin, God promises a deliverer. In the same breath God judges Satan and promises to rescue his fallen people. To the serpent, God declares, 'I will put enmity between you and the woman, and between your offspring and her offspring; he shall bruise your head, and you shall bruise his heel.' (Genesis 3:15) In other words, a day would come when there would come one who would be born of a woman, who would enter battle with the devil, and who would ultimately deliver the devil a fatal blow. This was not God working out a plan B, this was God revealing his eternal purpose to rescue and redeem his people. This is why the last book in the Bible speaks about 'the Lamb slain from the foundation of the world.' (Revelation 13:8) and this is why the apostles declared that Jesus who was 'delivered up according to the definite plan and foreknowledge of God, you crucified and killed by the hands of lawless men.' (Acts 2:23)

Saviour and Substitute

It is clear that God planned the cross, but what was the purpose of the cross? What was the cross designed to achieve? The prophet Isaiah was clear; God's deliverer would act as a saviour and a substitute: 'But he was wounded for our transgressions; he was crushed for our iniquities ... by his knowledge shall the righteous one, my servant, make many to be accounted righteous' (Isaiah 53:5,11). The concept of sacrifice and substitute runs right through the entire Bible. We see it in the sacrificial lamb of the Exodus, we see it in the Old Testament blood sacrifices, and we see it fulfilled in Jesus, 'Behold, the Lamb of God, who takes away the sin of the world!' (John 1:29)

Because the world is stained with sin, the cross is stained with the blood of a saviour. The death of Jesus is the price of our redemption. The wages of sin for humanity was death, and it is the death of the righteous Son of God which has paid the price to buy us back from the shackles of sin. Peter reminds us,

> knowing that you were ransomed from the futile ways inherited from your forefathers, not with perishable things such as silver or gold, but with the precious blood of Christ, like that of a lamb without blemish or spot. (1 Peter 1:18–19)

Jesus' death is not only the price of our redemption and ransom; it is the means by which we are delivered from the wrath of God, this is why Paul tells us that Jesus was 'put forward as a propitiation by his blood'. In other words, God's justice is fulfilled in the death of Jesus. The Old

Testament law was clear, without the sacrifice of blood, there is no forgiveness:

> For the life of the flesh is in the blood, and I have given it for you on the altar to make atonement for your souls, for it is the blood that makes atonement by the life. (Leviticus 17:11)

It's great that many contemporary evangelicals are passionate about changing the world and giving hope to the hopeless, but it's tragic that contemporary evangelicals have lost sight of the nature of the hopelessness and the true message of hope. True evangelism must confront people with sin and present people with a saviour. People are not just victims in need of help; they are rebels in need of pardon. The gospel does not just call us to make better lifestyle decisions; the gospel calls us to repent.

The cross is counter cultural. To the liberal, it's 'ghastly theology'; to the progressive evangelical, it's too negative; to the prosperity preacher it's too void of earthly benefits; but to the person being saved, it is the power of God, 'For the message of the cross is foolishness to those who are perishing, but to us who are being saved it is the power of God.' (1 Corinthians 1:18)

Evangelicals need to get specific. What do we mean when we say we want to see people transformed by Christ? What do we mean when we say we want people to discover the hope of the gospel? In the current context, these words have become devoid of meaning. There is a great need to not only preach the gospel, but to explain the gospel. Evangelicals need to move beyond soundbites and buzzwords, and start getting down to the nitty gritty with people. True Christianity is more than a meme, the message of the cross has substance and depth and it should be communicated in a way that reflects this fact. Granted, we live in a culture that revels on the soundbite, but our call is not to reflect the culture but to raise the standard. We need to rediscover the reality that, outside of Christ, all of us are bound for hell. All have sinned, all are under judgement, and all need to be saved. The only way to be saved is through faith in Christ as our sole substitute and saviour, and the only way for people to believe is to hear, and the only way they will hear is if we tell them. To be faithful to the message of the cross will cost us; it will cost us our reputations, but the eternal rewards will far outweigh the temporal inconveniences.

The Bible, from start to finish is about the cross of Christ. There is a river of blood which runs from Genesis to Revelation. The church's dual sacraments of baptism and communion speak of the death of Christ and the blood that cleanses. In the Garden, God promised a serpent crushing rescuer, the prophets predicted a suffering saviour, and the apostles preached a crucified Christ—let us do likewise.

And I, when I came to you, brothers, did not come proclaiming to you the testimony of God with lofty speech or wisdom. For I decided to know nothing among you except Jesus Christ and him crucified. And I was with you in weakness and in fear and much trembling, and my speech and my message were not in plausible words of wisdom, but in demonstration of the Spirit and of power, so that your faith might not rest in the wisdom of men but in the power of God. 1 Corinthians 2:1–5)

Chapter Eleven: Radical Church

The western church is in crisis. The cultural shift from Christendom to secularism has affected the church's sense of belonging, identity and purpose. For too long the western church has derived its identity from its position and power within the culture. A loss of position and power has caused the church to develop an identity crisis. The church is unsure of who it is, why it exists and what it is supposed to do. Many churches are dying and wrestling with issues concerning institutional survival—the question for many is, *how can we preserve a seat at the cultural table in the 21st century?*

A passing glance at many of the bestselling books on ecclesiology (the theology of the church) proves beyond a doubt the current crises. The titles are revealing: '*Autopsy of a deceased church: 12 ways to keep yours alive*'; '*Reimagining Church: Pursuing the dream of organic Christianity*'; '*Resurgence: will Christianity have a funeral or a future?*'; '*Permission granted to do church differently in the 21st century' 'How to multiply your church'* and *'church marketing 101: Preparing your church for greater growth'.* These titles are nothing more than a snapshot. But the snapshot gives us an accurate picture of the problems facing the 21st century church. The church is wrestling with who it is, why it exists and what it is designed to do. At least, thinking churches are concerned with these questions, many other churches are simply interested in keeping the machine running, and consequently institutional survival has become more important than Biblical faithfulness and missional engagement. A leading Free Church minister recently summed up the situation by saying, 'Too much of the British church is without God, without Christ and without the Holy Spirit.'[1]

A Church facing many challenges

Culturally, the emerging dominance of secularism, humanism, relativism, and, materialism has forced the church towards the side-lines. It's not that people don't believe in morality anymore, it simply that morality has been redefined—we can now be good without God. The church for many people is an outdated and irrelevant institution. Within the church, liberal theology, pragmatism and the schismatic nature of Protestantism has caused the church to plant the seeds of its own destruction. Consequently, by and large, the church is a dying institution that is desperately seeking to re-invent itself.

There are both positive and negative aspects to the current situation. On the one hand there is a new opportunity for the church to refocus its priorities, ditch its baggage and re-embrace its Biblical identity, purpose and mission. This, in many ways, is the responsibility of every church in every generation, the reformers referred to this as *Semper Reformanda*—the church is always reformed and always reforming. In order to put *Semper Reformanda* into practice, the church, in every generation must always evaluate its beliefs and practices in light of Scripture and amend them accordingly. On the other hand, the current context is a breeding ground for opportunists, mavericks, and heretics to rebrand the church in their own image.

The current conflict between the need for ongoing Biblical reformation and the move towards unbiblical innovation has created a sharp divide within the church. Some churches have responded by choosing a path of fundamentalist isolation and others are embracing cultural engagement to the point where the distinction between the church and the world becomes almost non-existent. One side is strong on the need to be faithful to truth and holiness but is neglecting the call to be 'salt and light'; the others are seeking to be 'all things to all men' whilst forgetting the reason *why*, in seeking to attract the world, they have become like the world. When our seeker sensitive philosophy causes us to turn out the light in order to attract people in darkness, we have lost the point of mission. Identifying with darkness, in an attempt to reach into the darkness, is not cultural relevance, it is Biblical compromise.

Belonging—where does the church fit?

For too long the western church has occupied a throne and has abandoned the cross. The church has reigned as king instead of bowing as a servant. It has sought prestige in place of poverty. As Christendom collapses, and the church continues to lose its cultural privileges of power, position and influence, it can perhaps rediscover its heavenly responsibilities of servanthood, humility and sacrifice. As the church loses its right to lead through legislation and law, it can rediscover how to lead with a basin and towel as it rediscovers the call to wash society's feet.

Christendom created a culture which was shaped by the Judeo-Christian worldview—in other words, many basic morals were taken for granted. The Law of God was once embedded in the law of the land; this is no longer the case. In one sense this is tragic for society, it is never good for any culture or society to reject or neglect the universal, moral laws of God. The Word of God is clear: 'Righteousness exalts a nation, but sin is a reproach to any people.' Proverbs (14:34) However, on the other hand, the changing cultural context places the church in a position that is far closer to the early Christians. They did not have the privilege of living in a nation that was shaped by Christian values yet they turned the world upside down.

The new context means that the values of churches, and Christians, no longer reflect the mainstream values. At one time, Christianized values were considered mainstream, even divorce was considered a social taboo in the 50s and 60s in many Scottish communities. However, as the protestant and catholic strongholds have lost their influence, humanism and relativism have taken their place. Consequently, true Biblical values are now radical. Christian beliefs and values are now counter-culture. The death of Christendom means that Christians need to rediscover what it means to be the church. Christendom has made it difficult for churches to understand what it means to be 'sojourners and exiles' (1 Peter 2:11). The new context, on the other hand, brings home this reality. As state morality continues to depart from Biblical foundations it is becoming clearer that this world is not our home.

Jesus is Lord

The early Christians quickly discovered the cost of discipleship. For people living under the rule of Rome the privileges were many, and to enjoy these privileges the cost was simple, all a person had to do was acknowledge that 'Caesar was Lord'. If a person would acknowledge Caesar as sole-supreme ruler, all would be well. However, to refuse to do this would be to risk persecution, punishment and death. The cost was clear, to confess that Jesus is Lord, was to dethrone Caesar and invoke the wrath of the state. And this is exactly what happened. The early Christians were thrown in prison, fed to lions, sawn in half, and dipped in tar, hung from Nero's palace and burned alive as human candles.

Time and time again, throughout history, and in various cultures, the state has emerged as a false god. It has arisen as the sole-authority and conscience of the people. This is currently the case in places like China and Korea. Western

Christians have normally enjoyed the luxuries that come with living in a Christianized culture, but these days are coming to an end.

As the church of Christ loses its privileges, it enters the process of renegotiating its relationship with the state. Christians are not anarchists, but neither should they be mindless conformists. It's one thing when the rulers of nations forget that there is a higher authority above them, but it is another thing entirely when the church forgets that there is a higher authority than the state. We must remember two things, firstly God is sovereign over all things, and secondly, God has given the governors and rulers their authority. Consequently, Christians are called to honour, respect, pray for and serve the government.

Let every person be subject to the governing authorities. For there is no authority except from God, and those that exist have been instituted by God. 2 Therefore whoever resists the authorities resists what God has appointed, and those who resist will incur judgement. 3 For rulers are not a terror to good conduct, but to bad. Would you have no fear of the one who is in authority? Then do what is good, and you will receive his approval, 4 for he is God's servant for your good. But if you do wrong, be afraid, for he does not bear the sword in vain. For he is the servant of God, an avenger who carries out God's wrath on the wrongdoer. 5 Therefore one must be in subjection, not only to avoid God's wrath but also for the sake of conscience. 6 For because of this you also pay taxes, for the authorities are ministers of God, attending to this very thing. 7 Pay to all what is owed to them: taxes to whom taxes are owed, revenue to whom revenue is owed, respect to whom respect is owed, honour to whom honour is owed. (Romans 14:1–7)

The Word of God is clear; Christians are not to embrace the perspective of anarchists, or endorse an anti-establishment attitude. The church is called to celebrate all that is good in government.

However, the church is also called to be true to God and his Word. When the state usurps the role of God and seeks to bind the conscience of people, the church has a moral obligation to stand fast for truth—no matter the cost. When the state begins to redefine what is right and wrong, and when the laws of the land force the church to disobey the laws of God, the church must hold fast to the words of Jesus when he said, 'Render to Caesar the things that are Caesar's, and to God the things that are God's.' (Mark 12:17) In other words, where the laws of the land do not conflict with Scripture, Christians should obey the laws of the land, but where the laws of the land force the church to disobey the Word of God; the church must obey God over and above the laws of the land. It is obedience to this principle that took Jesus to the cross where he was condemned as a criminal who had committed treason. It is this principle that has led multitudes of Christians to be persecuted, imprisoned and put to death throughout the centuries, and it is this principle that western Christians must rediscover and apply whilst society shifts towards a secular dystopia.

Meaningless Mission

The new context provides the church with both challenge and opportunity. Churches are no longer representative of a mainstream world view; they must recognize the fact that they are simply one voice amidst many other organizations and groups within their communities. However, like other groups and organizations, they have the opportunity to get involved and active within their communities. Consequently there is still a role for the church in the political, educational, media, and community spheres. However, there is also a danger here; the danger is that the church redefines its identity in order to fit harmoniously with the new global values and ethos. In other words, if the church simply accepts, uncritically, the values, priorities and language of the secular culture—the church will lose its prophetic voice. Martin Luther King Junior once said that the church is 'not merely a thermometer that recorded the ideas and principles of popular opinion'; but is 'a thermostat that transformed the mores of society.' When the church adopts the ethos and values of the age, we no longer function as a thermostat, we're simply a thermometer that reflects the moral temperature of the world around us.

I've observed this capitulation to the culture on numerous occasions, particularly when the church is given an opportunity to speak at school assemblies, or parliament, or through some other media platform. Ministers, or representatives of the church, instead of confidently speaking from Biblical convictions, will instead attempt to reflect the priorities, values and language of the culture. Consequently, very often, devotional and reflective talks at parliament are nothing more than politically correct platitudes; school assemblies are reduced to ambiguous moralism and media opportunities become a concoction of compromise cowardice.

Chapter Twelve: Radical Builders

Judgement is a time of shaking. When God judges a nation, his church, or our individual lives, the judgement is often designed to reveal our foundations. If our foundations are secure, we will stand secure in the midst of judgement, if our foundations are faulty, we will crumble. Over the last number of decades, as the old mainline denominations have slipped into irrelevance, many new churches and church networks have emerged. Very often these churches are pioneered by strong charismatic individuals with huge vision and gifting. We hear stories of churches which began in someone's home only to expand and grow into the latest mega church. The church grows; it becomes a brand, develops a logo, and spreads its slogans through effective use of social media. Very often these churches will rise like a huge wave, but, like the wave, they also come crashing down. A particular example of this is the Mark Driscoll phenomena. Driscoll's church, Mars Hill, emerged as a leading light in the young, restless and reformed movement. The church was growing, books were being published, conferences being hosted and young leaders were looking to Mars Hill for leadership guidance, and then almost overnight, the whole edifice came crumbling down. The problem? The church was built on the wrong foundation.

Many contemporary churches look good on the surface, they have exciting vision, they are attracting many people in the 20–40s categories; they have excellent children and young people's services; their worship team are awesome and their Sunday services are slick—how can there be a problem?

Discernment is a missing virtue in today's church. Today, if it is big, exciting, and drawing a crowd the assumption is that it must be good. The fact that many professing Christians look at things in this way is clear evidence that we have departed from Biblical thinking. Throughout Scripture it is clear, that in God's economy, things are often reversed. In God's economy, it is the weak that are strong, the poor who are rich, the foolish that are called, and the insignificant who are given value and dignity. The church-growth movement has lost sight of this important fact. A large, richly-resourced, active and engaging church is no guarantee that the church is healthy. An enchanting edifice is no guarantee that the church is built on the right foundations or that the church is being built with the right materials. In the end the whole thing may come crashing down when God comes to judge the quality of the work.

¹⁰ By the grace God has given me, I laid a foundation as a wise builder, and someone else is building on it. But each one should build with care. ¹¹ For no one can lay any

foundation other than the one already laid, which is Jesus Christ. [12] If anyone builds on this foundation using gold, silver, costly stones, wood, hay or straw, [13] their work will be shown for what it is, because the Day will bring it to light. It will be revealed with fire, and the fire will test the quality of each person's work. [14] If what has been built survives, the builder will receive a reward. [15] If it is burned up, the builder will suffer loss but yet will be saved—even though only as one escaping through the flames. (1Corinthians 3:10–15)

Paul is crystal clear, the foundation for the church must be Christ, and Christ alone. However many contemporary churches continue to build and grow their churches on human vision, ambition and personality. Consequently, many contemporary churches are nothing more than a monument to the glory of their founders. When this happens, discipleship is radically altered, and so is the Christian ministry. In a Biblical church, the pastor's role is to:

> equip the saints for the work of ministry, for building up the body of Christ, until we all attain to the unity of the faith and of the knowledge of the Son of God, to mature manhood, to the measure of the stature of the fullness of Christ. (Ephesians 4:12–13)

In contrast, churches that are birthed out of human ambition and vision are led by leaders who use church members to fulfil their personal vision and agenda. In this context, faithfulness to Christ means loyalty to the leader, and commitment to implementing the leader's vision. Whereas in Biblical churches, true pastors are concerned with seeing church members grow in Christ. Consequently, there is a real danger, in our current evangelical climate of *en masse* church planting, missional pioneering, and church marketing, that we are deceiving ourselves into thinking we are building the kingdom of God when in reality we are building our own empires. One of the most haunting teachings of Jesus is directed, not to unbelievers, but to those who think they are doing great things for the Kingdom of God.

> Not everyone who says to me, 'Lord, Lord,' will enter the kingdom of heaven, but the one who does the will of my Father who is in heaven. On that day many will say to me, 'Lord, Lord, did we not prophesy in your name, and cast out demons in your name, and do many mighty works in your name?' And then will I declare to them, 'I never knew you; depart from me, you workers of lawlessness.' (Matthew 7:21–23)

The message is clear, on the day of Judgement, what will count, is not how dynamic our ministry was, but how authentic our ministry was. Is our ministry a genuine outworking of the Lordship of Christ over our lives, or is our ministry simply the expression of our own narcissistic notions?

A church with the right government

In the UK, during the Protestant Reformation, most churches defined themselves in simple theological and geographical terms: *The* Church of Scotland; *The* Church of Ireland; *The* Church of England. It was all very simple, they defined themselves simply in terms of *who* they were (*the* church) and *where* they were (their national location).

The reformers did not see themselves as schismatic, as far as they were concerned, Rome's excommunication of the reformers, and its condemnation of the gospel meant Rome had declared itself an apostate church, consequently the Protestant Church understood itself as *the* church reformed. The reformation churches were developed out of serious theological reflection, not only about doctrines relating to salvation, but also doctrines of the church. The reformation emerged because it was believed that the church had lost its way in two of the most essential areas— the message of salvation and the nature of the church.

However, the reformation was not a complete success. With the Bible in the hands of the people, many individuals arose with their own personal interpretation of the Scriptures. Splinter groups emerged, new denominations were established, and independent churches spread like wild-fire—each group claiming to hold to the true teachings of Scripture.

It's interesting to observe how the churches throughout the period from the reformation, to the present day, have defined themselves. The churches have shifted from emphasizing who they are in simple, and essential terms— the Church of Scotland, to then identifying themselves in terms of their specific governmental peculiarities. So, the Church of England, in Scotland is known as the Episcopal Church (emphasizing its unique position on Bishops); the disruption in the Church of Scotland gives birth to the Free Church of Scotland (emphasizing their conviction about the church being free from state control); then Congregational Churches emerge, again emphasizing their particular commitment to congregational government. So the trend shifts from being the church, in a nation, and a locality, to being primarily identified in ecclesiological terms. In other words, their government defined their identity.

However, as the schisms and increased and continued, churches began to gather around various theological particularities. So we see the development of 'Baptist', 'Holiness', 'Brethren', 'Pentecostal' and 'Apostolic' churches. This trend continued throughout the 20th century, but a significant shift took place as the church approached the millennium.

The cultural tide was shifting. The world, so it seemed, had no more time for religious conflict and division. Church splits, and the splitting of theological hairs, were a huge turn off to a world that was becoming increasingly pluralistic, and relativistic. The UK had witnessed the full extent of the ugliness of religious conflict through the Catholic and Protestant divide; consequently there was no interest in the various in-house fighting of the emerging splinter churches. At the end of the day, what did all these church distinctives mean to the lost? Absolutely nothing.

The reformation left Protestant groups with an identity problem. Churches, it seems, were defined primarily what they were against. Non-Roman Catholic Churches, it seemed, were forever haunted by the ghost of negativity, by definition the churches could not escape the fact that they were *protestant*. Further, even their own theological distinctive was usually a reaction to some other church group from whom they had split. So the Holiness movements were a reaction to the nominalism of the state churches, the brethren were a reaction to the ecclesiastical hierarchy of the state churches and the Pentecostal churches were a reaction to the coldness of conservativism. No matter who the church group is, they existed as a group as a reaction to another group—and this inevitably taints the church with a degree of negativity.

Consequently, the 21st century churches have attempted to address this issue of negativity. New churches, define themselves in positive, and theologically neutral terms, and old churches are rebranding and renaming their local churches. In the nineties it was fashionable to call your church 'community' church, with the only other identifier being the name of the locality e.g. Paisley Community Church, or a positive theological term e.g. Grace Community Church. Whilst some churches are still following this trend, in recent years, the trend is towards innovative, creative, and theologically neutral (or ambiguous) church names. So we are seeing the emergence of the church brand where churches are adopting slick names, logos, and slogans. The motivation for the rebrand is often understood in missional terms. The church is attempting to help the non-Christian culture understand what they are for, not what they are against. However the methods being adopted are that of the market place. Consequently, the question needs to be asked, if churches are trading their theological identities, for positive missional identities, and rebranding themselves through the language and methods of the corporate market place, *are churches competing against each other like their secular counterparts?* If theological differences are no longer the issues which define and divide us, are our various churches with their own unique trendy and missional brands, partners in the mission field or competitors in the market place?

The emergence of the *brand-defined* church is a symptom of a major shift which has taken in place in how the church understands church leaders. The traditional pastor who prays for the flock, visits the flock, and preaches to the flock, is no longer in vogue, the current need is for visionaries, pioneers, and entrepreneurs. The generic theological term for this new style of leadership is *apostolic*, although more conservative churches may reject the terminology whilst embracing the methodology. Whether the term apostolic is embraced, or not, the trend is evident, the new style of church requires a new style of leadership. In a context of church decline, low-level church commitment, and financial difficulty, the church is desperate for leaders who can cast a vision, gather a crowd and raise finance.

Whilst we must recognize the need for leaders who are able to lead churches missionally, we must also recognize the weaknesses of the current trends. As churches redefine themselves in positive, missional terms, and neglect foundational theological issues, we need to understand what is happening. The church is adopting a pragmatic approach to teaching and practice. Many contemporary churches are nothing more than positive, feel-good clubs, effectively marketed and managed by a charismatic leader. There is very little difference between contemporary youth ministry methods and values, and the methods and values of contemporary evangelical churches. Many 'cutting edge' churches are simply glorified youth-groups. This has huge implications for not only the message of the church, but also the very nature of the church. Consequently, the contemporary church may be the fastest growing section of the church, but the question needs to be asked, what kind of church is it producing? If we examine the new church phenomena against the Biblical criteria; we shall quickly notice that the new church movement is leading the church back to a pre-reformation state.

Protestant Popes

One of the central truths that the reformation restored was the headship of Christ. Under the Roman Catholic Church rule, human leadership had eclipsed the headship of Christ—this was most fully seen in the office of the Pope. Since the reformation, the reformed churches have been zealous to maintain the headship of Christ. As far as reformed churches are concerned, it is Christ, not the state, or the pastor who is the head of the church. As we see churches shooting up like wild flowers, we need to ask the question, *whose churches are these?* Are these churches of Christ, or are they simply the religious organizations of men?

The headship of Christ, over his church, is no hyper-spiritual doctrine. It has a very real and practical outworking. Accompanying the doctrine of the Headship of Christ is the doctrine of the Priesthood of all believers, and with the priesthood of believers is the doctrine of Biblical church government. Whilst church government is a doctrine which reformed believers have disagreed over (there are reformed believers in Presbyterian, Baptist and Episcopalian contexts) it has to be said that the new apostolically-led churches have the weakest kind of church government imaginable. The apostolic model may empower the visionary to plough new fields at great speed, unhindered by dodgy deacons and cautious elders but it ultimately disempowers the church. In many apostolic contexts, there is a tendency for the headship of Christ to be eclipsed by the headship of man, and the priesthood of all believers gives way to a hierarchical system.

The new apostolic approach to church government places a man and his vision at the head of the church. If the man's church grows into a church planting movement, the man becomes the head of the movement. In this context, even where eldership is implemented, it is often deficient. In the apostolic context, the 'pastor' is 'the first amongst equals' which means that the eldership become a kind of middle-management. In this situation, the lead pastor sets the direction, the elders implement his vision, and the congregation conforms. Very often, in apostolic settings, congregations will have no say in who their elders are, or, if their minister is moving on, who their new minister will be. These decisions are made by the leading apostolic figure. All of this should concern Biblically-minded believers greatly; the church is not our play-thing, it is the House of the living God. The church does not belong to us, it belongs to Jesus.

Regarding the Headship of Christ, the Westminster Confession simply states, 'There is no other head of the

Church but the Lord Jesus Christ: nor can the Pope of Rome in any sense be head thereof.'[1] Whilst the Pope is singled out, it does not only apply to the pope. The Headship of Christ is the fundamental confession that 'Jesus Christ is Lord', consequently there can be no rivals to Christ's headship. When the headship of Christ is usurped by state, or religious authorities, the church ceases to be a true church. Consequently, a recovery of the Headship of Christ is extremely relevant today as both secular leaders, and religious figures, seek to dominate the beliefs, and practices of the church.

A Right Confession

If the evangelical church is ever to recover its Biblical identity, purpose and practices, it needs to return to a Biblical Confession of Faith. Whilst most churches still claim to believe that the Bible is the Word of God, without a Confession of Faith this belief becomes meaningless. Scripture is always interpreted, but the question is whose interpretation carries the greatest authority? The pastor's? The denomination's? Or the individual's? The emergence of apostolic leaders, and the widespread tendency towards individualism, has had a serious impact upon the unity of the church. Consequently, Scripture has lost its authority. In many churches, Christians are either blindly following the interpretation of a strong leader, or stubbornly following their own individualistic interpretations. Either way, the outcome is the same; the authority of Scripture is undermined.

Church Confessions are not an addition to Scripture,

they are (or should be) a summary of Scripture. The Confession is subordinate to Scripture, it is not above it. However, critics of church confessions are concerned that church confessions undermine the centrality of Scripture, but the irony is, it is our neglect of Church Confessions which compromise the authority of Scripture. A pastor friend once said to me, 'The problem with subordinate standards is that the Bible becomes subordinate!' Whilst this is something that could happen (and it is for this reason the church must always be open to revising their confessions) the reality is it is the lack of a clear Biblical Confession that causes the Bible to become subordinate to the imaginations of apostles, or the opinions of men.

The effectiveness of Church Confessions can easily be demonstrated. Where do we find the greatest faithfulness to Scripture, the gospel, and the essential doctrines of the faith? It is surely amongst the churches that have been faithful to preserve their commitment to a Biblical Church Confession. Where do we find the greatest chaos, and confusion? It is amongst the churches that have neglected, or rejected church Confessions. However, this is not to make the case that a church can only be faithful if it adopts a reformed Presbyterian, or reformed Baptist Confession of Faith. Whilst these documents could be of great service to the greater evangelical world, the starting place for most evangelicals must be to return to the Word of God. In addition to this churches should be encouraged to rediscover their own historical Statements of Faith and ecclesiastical convictions. In other words, Baptists should seek to rediscover what it means to be Baptist again, and the same is true for Pentecostals, Congregationalists and Independents. In other words, there needs to be a fresh priority given to the Scriptures, church confessions, ecclesiology and doctrine.

Building a Radical Community

The church was not meant to be some religious-social club for infants and the elderly. The church is the redeemed community of the King. Those who profess faith in Christ are incorporated into God's redeemed people. This redeemed people, in turn become the vehicle through which God is redeeming others to himself. The church is not at home in this world. We look forward to the world that it is to come. Whilst we are here, we seek to bless the world, and to lead the world to Christ—but we are never at home here, and the world is never at home with us. Jesus Christ is the sole Head of the church, and because of this, Christians have dual citizenship. We seek to live God-honouring lives, in submission to the governments of our lands—but our allegiance only goes so far. When the state begins to intrude upon the consciences of Christians, Christians are called to humbly remain faithful to Christ, even when that means conflict with the laws of the land. As has historically happened, time and time again, when the State attempts to silence the church, the church must respond with, 'Whether it is right in the sight of God to listen to you rather than to God, you must judge' (Acts 4:19).

As the state increasingly seeks to define and politicize identity, morality, and religious practice; the church and Christians will find themselves in a crisis. Who will we obey, the State, or Jesus? When God's law for sexual activity says one thing, and the law of the land says another, who will the church listen to? When God's Word says preach the gospel to all people, and call each one to repentance, and the society interprets evangelism as a hate crime—who will the church obey? These questions are no longer hypothetical scenarios; they are already the issues that Christians are facing today.

The same is true for the values, trends, and priorities of the wider culture. When the church substitutes Biblical truths, for cultural values, the church loses its Biblical identity and purpose. When the church tries to become like the world, in order to win the world, it's already lost the battle. We cannot profess 'Jesus is Lord' whilst confessing that 'Caesar is Lord'. Likewise we can't seek the approval of the culture and Christ simultaneously—as Jesus said, we can't serve two masters.

As Christians we must never allow our faith to be redefined by the state or the culture. As soon as we do, we have compromised the gospel, sold our souls, denied our Lord, and trampled underfoot our crucified saviour. We are now in the situation where if we want to be faithful, we will be by definition, radical. As the world grows darker, the faithful church will shine brighter. As Christian opposition grows more extreme, the faithful church will rediscover what it is to be the radical church.

Notes

Introduction

1. http://www.express.co.uk/news/uk/651684/judge-christian-sacked-gay-couple-man-and-woman-richard-page-magistrate-adopted-child
2. http://www.dailyrecord.co.uk/news/politics/new-tory-equality-minister-voted-5685337#vhDt5MBFtMb57Jtj.97
3. http://www.churchofscotland.org.uk/news_and_events/news/recent/kirk_votes_in_favour_of_allowing_ministers_in_same_sex_civil_partnerships

Chapter 1

1. We are talking here metaphorically about the concept of God; we are not talking about God in a literal sense.
2. http://www.secularism.org.uk/only38ofbritonsbelieveingod.html
3. http://www.telegraph.co.uk/news/general-election-2015/11516804/David-Cameron-declares-Britain-is-still-a-Christian-country.html
4. http://www.secularism.org.uk/only38ofbritonsbelieveingod.html
5. *Transforming Scotland: the state of Christianity, faith, and the church in Scotland*, Barna.
6. Alister McGrath, *The Dawkins Delusion? Atheist Fundamentalism and the Denial of the Divine* (IVP 2007), 19–20.
7. http://www.skeptical-science.com/essays/science-religion-richard-dawkins/
8. https://www.youtube.com/watch?v=H9UKTuuTHEg
9. https://www.facebook.com/atrbox/?fref=ts
10. http://www.dailymail.co.uk/news/article-2312813/Richard-Dawkins-Forcing-religion-children-child-abuse-claims-atheist-professor.html

11. http://educateagainsthate.com/parents/how-do-people-become-radicalised-4/

12. http://christianconcern.com/our-concerns/employment/christian-nhs-worker-loses-appeal-over-freedom-to-talk-to-a-muslim-colleague?utm_content=buffer87811&utm_medium=social&utm_source=facebook.com&utm_campaign=buffer

13. http://www.eauk.org/current-affairs/news/ofsted-chief-confirms-sunday-schools-will-need-to-register-under-anti-extremism-proposals.cfm

14. http://www.telegraph.co.uk/news/religion/11344228/Europe-is-becoming-a-no-God-zone.html

Chapter 2

1. http://www.ssa.natcen.ac.uk/media-centre/latest-press-releases/ssa-2015-two-thirds-of-religious-scots-don-t-attend-services.aspx

Chapter 3

1. http://www.reformed.org/documents/index.html?mainframe=http://www.reformed.org/documents/BelgicConfession.html

2. http://www.reformed.org/documents/index.html?mainframe=http://www.reformed.org/documents/BelgicConfession.html

3. http://nae.net/what-is-an-evangelical/

4. An example of the detailed core doctrines which marked early evangelicalism, can be seen in the historic Evangelical Alliance (EA) Statement of Faith:

"Evangelical Christians accept the revelation of the triune God given in the Scriptures of the Old and New Testaments and confess the historic faith of the Gospel therein set forth. They here assert doctrines which they regard as crucial to the understanding of the faith, and which should issue in mutual love, practical Christian service and evangelical concern.

* The sovereignty and grace of God the Father, God the Son and God the Holy Spirit in creation, providence, revelation, redemption and final judgement.

* The divine inspiration of the Holy Scripture and its consequent entire trustworthiness and supreme authority in all matters of faith and conduct.

* The universal sinfulness and guilt of fallen man, making him subject to God's wrath and condemnation.

* The substitutionary sacrifice of the incarnate Son of God as the sole all-sufficient ground of redemption from the guilt and power of sin, and from its eternal consequences.

* The justification of the sinner solely by the grace of God through faith in Christ crucified and risen from the dead.

* The illuminating, regenerating, indwelling and sanctifying work of God the Holy Spirit.

* The priesthood of all believers, who form the universal Church, the Body of which Christ is the Head and which is committed by his command to the proclamation of the Gospel throughout the world.

* The expectation of the personal, visible return of the Lord Jesus Christ in power and glory.

The opening paragraph of the Statement of Faith stresses several essential convictions. Firstly, it declares that, 'Evangelical Christians accept the revelation of the triune God given in the Scriptures of the Old and New Testaments.' In other words, evangelicals base their understanding of God on the Bible, which they believe to be the 'revelation' of God. This means that God has made himself known through the words of Holy Scripture. Secondly, it declares that evangelicals, 'Confess the historic faith of the Gospel therein set forth.' In other words, their faith is not some novel innovative expression of Christianity; it is the historic gospel which was delivered to the apostles by Jesus Christ and by revelation of the Holy Spirit. Thirdly, they: 'Assert doctrines which they regard as crucial to the understanding of the faith.' By this, they are declaring that the doctrines set forth in the statement are essential for understanding the Christian faith. If a person wants to understand Christianity, he must understand these doctrines. Fourthly, these doctrines should, 'Issue in mutual love, practical Christian service and evangelical concern.' In other words, the doctrines are not intended to be abstract theories which bear no practical relevance. They are the very means by which Christians will be motivated towards love, service and concern for people who are lost.

At this point it should be clear that early evangelicalism was primarily concerned with the knowledge of God as revealed in the Bible; a historical confession of faith; the importance of doctrine, practical Christian service and concern for the lost. For the evangelical, these areas were woven together and not one of them was considered dispensable. This is not the case within evangelicalism today.

5.   Bebbington argues for four marks: Conversionism: the belief that lives need to be transformed through a "born-again" experience and a lifelong process of following Jesus; Activism: the expression and demonstration of the gospel in missionary and social reform efforts; Biblicism: a high regard for and obedience to the Bible as the ultimate authority and Crucicentrism: a stress on the sacrifice of Jesus Christ on the cross as making possible the redemption of humanity.

6.   Bebbington's definition of evangelicalism, whilst being widely

accepted by many evangelicals, is in many ways insufficient. However, even by this minimalist definition, evangelicalism is falling short of these very basic criteria. This in itself shows just how serious the evangelical crisis is. Broad evangelicals, along with the reformed, have historically agreed that the Bible and the Cross are essential marks of an evangelical, but these essential marks are being side-lined in today's evangelicalism.

7. http://nae.net/what-is-an-evangelical/
8. http://www.eauk.org/connect/about-us/what-is-an-evangelical.cfm
9. Transforming Scotland
10. http://nae.net/what-is-an-evangelical/
11. https://blogs.thegospelcoalition.org/erikraymond/2016/02/17/common-evangelical-attacks-against-sola-scriptura/
12. https://humanism.org.uk/humanism/how-humanist-are-you/

Chapter 4
1. https://humanism.org.uk/humanism/
2. http://www.reformed.org/documents/wcf_with_proofs/
3. http://www.theguardian.com/commentisfree/belief/2009/dec/31/evangelicals-god-america
4. Gordon Fee and Simon Chan are two leading Pentecostal scholars who have identified unbiblical trends and patterns within the charismatic movement. Lee Grady and Michael Brown have also attempted to correct the movement from various excesses. Also, the late US Pastor, David Wilkerson, and the late Scottish pastor Hugh B Black have written and spoken about errors and extremes within the movement.
5. http://www.reformed.org/documents/wcf_with_proofs/

Chapter 5
1. https://humanism.org.uk/campaigns/successful-campaigns/atheist-bus-campaign/
2. Blood Hound Gang, 'Aint nothing but mammals'
3. Madonna 'Material Girl'
4. Sam Sparro 'Black and Gold'
5. http://www.reformed.org/documents/wsc/index.html?_top=http://www.reformed.org/documents/WSC_frames.html
6. https://www.gov.uk/government/news/same-sex-marriage-becomes-law
7. http://www.christian.org.uk/wp-content/downloads/ashers-factsheet-jan16.pdf

8.   http://www.bbc.co.uk/news/uk-england-lancashire-15072408

9.   http://www.huffingtonpost.co.uk/2013/07/05/american-preacher-arreste_n_3549537.html

Chapter 6

1.   https://www.thegospelcoalition.org/article/we-are-all-messy-rosaria-butterfield-on-loving-our-gay-and-lesbian-friends

2.   https://www.thegospelcoalition.org/article/we-are-all-messy-rosaria-butterfield-on-loving-our-gay-and-lesbian-friends

3.   http://www.telegraph.co.uk/news/2016/03/31/nicola-sturgeon-scots-to-be-allowed-to-change-gender-so-they-are/

4.   https://freechurch.org/news/moderator-writes-to-nicola-sturgeon-urging-gender-fluid-debate

Chapter 7

1.   http://www.telegraph.co.uk/news/religion/11381589/Watch-Stephen-Fry-brands-God-utterly-utterly-evil.html

Chapter 8

2.   http://horshamhumanists.net/html/about.html

3.   https://www.wyhumanists.org.uk/humanism/humanism-in-more-depth/

4.   http://horshamhumanists.net/html/about.html

5.   https://www.wyhumanists.org.uk/humanism/humanism-in-more-depth/

6.   Sermon on Acts 13:13–49 published in 1904

Chapter 9

1.   http://www.patheos.com/blogs/adrianwarnock/2004/11/cosmic-child-abuse/

2.   Scott McKenna, Sermon, Sunday 1 March 2015, http://www.mayfieldsalisbury.org/index.php/extensions/sermons/message/inner-transformation

Chapter 10

1.   http://www.christiantoday.com/article/creflo.dollar.removes.facebook.post.which.claims.jesus.died.to.give.us.financial.prosperity/67092.htm

2. https://www.facebook.com/trinitybroadcastingnetwork/videos/1019834738053055/ Todd White

3. http://www.sermonindex.net/modules/newbb/viewtopic.php?topic_id=22556&forum=34

4. John Stott, *The Cross of Christ* (Downers Grove, IL, IVP, 1986), (Kindle Edition).

Chapter 11

1. http://www.christiantoday.com/article/too.much.of.the.british.church.is.without.god.without.christ.and.without.the.holy.spirit.just.like.rev/37126.htm

Chapter 12

1. http://www.reformed.org/documents/index.html?mainframe=http://www.reformed.org/documents/westminster_conf_of_faith.html